**TEACHER'S PET PUBLICATIONS**

LITPLAN TEACHER PACK
for
The Importance of Being Earnest
based on the book by
Oscar Wilde

Written by
Stephanie Polukis

© 2010 Teacher's Pet Publications

All Rights Reserved

Copyright Teacher's Pet Publications 2010

Only the student materials in this unit plan (such as worksheets, study questions, and test) may be reproduced multiple times for use in the purchaser's classroom.

For any additional copyright questions, contact Teacher's Pet Publications.

www.tpet.com

TABLE OF CONTENTS - *The Importance of Being Earnest*

About the Author	5
Introduction	7
Unit Objectives	9
Reading Assignment Sheet	10
Unit Outline	11
Study Questions (Short Answer)	15
Quiz/Study Questions (Multiple-Choice)	23
Pre-Reading Vocabulary Worksheets	35
Lesson One (Introductory Lesson)	51
Non-Fiction Assignment Sheet	60
Oral Reading Evaluation Sheet	61
Writing Assignment #1	63
Writing Evaluation Form	64
Project: Rewriting and Acting a Scene	69
Writing Assignment #2	92
Writing Assignment #3	94
Vocabulary Review Activities	97
Unit Review Activities	99
Unit Tests	104
Unit Resource Materials	150
Extra Writing Assignments/Discussion Questions	157
Quotations	159
Vocabulary Resource Materials	177

ABOUT THE AUTHOR

Oscar Wilde

Oscar Fingal O'Flahertie Wills Wilde was born on October 16, 1854, in Dublin, Ireland, to Sir William Wilde, a renowned ear and eye surgeon, and Jane Francesca Elgee, a writer and Irish nationalist.

After being home schooled by his mother until the age of nine, Oscar Wilde went to Portora Royal School in 1864. In 1871, he entered Trinity College in Dublin, and proved himself to be an outstanding student, winning the Berkeley Gold Medal, the highest award for students of classical studies. Shortly afterward, Wilde won a scholarship to Magdalen College in Oxford, where he continued his study of the classics and became part of the Aesthetic Movement. The Aesthetes believed that art should be valued based on beauty and the pleasure that can be derived from observing it, an idea that is discussed extensively in Wilde's novel *The Picture of Dorian Gray*. While at Magdalen College, Wilde won the 1878 Newdigate Prize for his poem "Ravenna." He graduated in 1878, with a double first (highest honors in two areas of study) in classical moderations and Literae Humaniores.

Wilde returned to Ireland after graduating from Magdalen. In Dublin, he met and fell in love with Florence Balcombe. When she did not return his affections and, instead, became engaged to Bram Stoker (author of *Dracula*), Wilde vowed to leave Ireland forever. He spent the next six years on a lecture tour that took him to London, Paris, and parts of the United States. While in London, Wilde met Constance Lloyd, the daughter of Queen's Counsel Horace Lloyd, and they married in 1884. Constance was given a generous allowance by her father, allowing her and Wilde to live a comfortably luxurious lifestyle. The couple had two sons, Cyril (1885) and Vyvyan (1886).

In 1891, Wilde was introduced to Lord Alfred Douglas, the third son of the 9th Marquess of Queensberry. The two became close companions, and although Wilde affirmed that he and Douglas were only emotionally and intellectually intimate, the Marquess suspected that Wilde was corrupting his son and encouraging him to engage in homosexual acts. The idea led the Marquess to enter Wilde's home, verbally harass him, and leave a visiting card at Wilde's club denouncing him as 'a posing sodomite.' Wilde responded to the latter action by accusing the Marquess of committing criminal libel. Although the Marquess was arrested, the conflict exposed Wilde's controversial relationship with Douglas to public censure. In 1895, Wilde was put on trial for homosexual acts. He was convicted of 'gross indecency' and sentenced to two years of hard labor.

Wilde was imprisoned in the Reading Gaol, where he composed a 50,000-word letter to Douglas, but was prohibited from sending it until his release. An abridged version of the letter was afterward published by Wilde's friend Robert Ross under the title *De Profundis* in 1905, and it has since been reproduced in various lengths until the final version was published by Wilde's son in 1965.

Following his release in May 1897, Wilde reunited with Douglas. He then spent the remainder of his life abroad. Wilde lived in relative poverty at the Hotel d'Alsace in Paris, until he died of cerebral meningitis on November 30, 1900.

Major Works

"The Happy Prince and Other Tales" (children's stories, 1888)
"The House of Pomegranates" (children's stories, 1892)
The Picture of Dorian Gray (novel, 1891)
Lady Windermere's Fan (play, 1892)
A Woman of No Importance (play, 1893)
An Ideal Husband (play, 1895)
The Importance of Being Earnest (play, 1895)
"The Ballad of Reading Gaol" (poem, 1898)

INTRODUCTION - *The Importance of Being Earnest*

This LitPlan has been designed to develop students' reading, writing, thinking, and language skills through exercises and activities related to *The Importance of Being Earnest*. It includes seventeen lessons, supported by extra resource materials.

The **introductory lesson** will familiarizes students with the Victorian Era and prompt them to make predictions about the themes and motifs in the play.

The **reading assignments** vary in length but are fairly short. Students have approximately 15 minutes of pre-reading work prior to each reading assignment. This pre-reading work involves reviewing the study questions for the assignment and doing vocabulary work for selected words students will encounter in their reading.

The **study guide questions** are fact-based; students can find the answers right in the text. The questions come in two formats: short answer or multiple-choice. To best use these materials, we recommend using the short answer questions as study guides for students (since answers will be more complete) and the multiple-choice questions for occasional quizzes.

The **vocabulary work** is intended to enrich students' vocabularies as well as to aid in their understanding of the play. Prior to each reading assignment, students will complete a two-part worksheet for selected vocabulary words in the upcoming reading assignment. Part I focuses on students' use of general knowledge and contextual clues by giving the sentence in which the word appears in the text. Students are to write down what they think the word means based on its usage. Part II reinforces comprehension of the words by having students match them to the correct definitions based on the words' contextual usage. Students should then have an understanding of the words when they encounter them in the text.

After each reading assignment, students will formulate answers for the study guide questions. Discussion of these questions serves as a **review** of the most important events and ideas presented in the reading assignments.

After students have read the play, the teacher can use the **vocabulary review** lesson to compile the vocabulary lists for the reading assignments and give students a review of the words they have studied.

There is a **Group Project and Presentation** in this unit. Students are asked to rewrite a section of the play so that the story is set in the present day, and the characters use colloquial speech. This project requires students to not only understand the basic essence of the plot and the characters, but also write in a way that makes the dialogue and action informative and entertaining. Furthermore, students will be asked to memorize their lines and perform their scenes in front of the class, thus practicing their public speaking skills.

There are three **writing assignments**, each with the purpose of informing, persuading, or expressing personal opinions. The first writing assignment asks students to research and report on Victorian marriage conventions. The second writing assignment asks students to explain how Oscar Wilde's life, the Victorian Era, and the Aesthetic Movement influenced the text. In the third assignment, students must use the play to develop an opinion about how personal identities are created and developed.

There is a **non-fiction reading assignment**. Students must read non-fiction articles, books, etc., to gather information about the themes discussed in the play.

The **review lesson** pulls together the entire unit. The teacher is given four or five choices of activities or games to use, all of which serve to review the information presented in the unit.

The **unit test** comes in two formats: multiple-choice or short answer. As a convenience, two different tests for each format have been included. There is also an advanced short answer unit test for higher-level students.

This unit includes additional **support materials**. The **Unit Resource Materials** section provides suggestions for **bulletin board ideas**, crossword and word search puzzles related to the play, and extra worksheets. This section also includes a list of **extra class activities** the teacher can choose from to enhance the unit or use as a substitution for an exercise the teacher might feel is inappropriate for his or her class. In addition, there are **extra discussion questions/writing assignments**. These questions focus on interpretation, critical analysis, and personal response, employing a variety of thinking skills and adding to the students' understanding of the play. **Answer keys** are located directly after the **reproducible student materials** throughout the unit. The **Vocabulary Resource Materials** section includes similar worksheets and games to reinforce the vocabulary words.

The **level** of this unit can be varied depending upon the criteria on which the individual assignments are graded, the teacher's expectations of his or her students in class discussions, and the formats chosen for the study guides, quizzes, and test. If the teacher has other ideas or wants to use other activities, they can usually easily be inserted prior to the review lesson.

The student materials may be reproduced for use in the teacher's classroom without infringement of copyrights. No other portion of this unit may be reproduced without the written consent of Teacher's Pet Publications, Inc.

UNIT OBJECTIVES - *The Importance of Being Earnest*

1. Students will research the historical context of the play and determine how the work is a product of its time period.

2. Students will determine to what extent the author's life influenced the play.

3. Students will compare and contrast characters in the play and identify characters who act as foils in the story.

4. Students will trace the motif of courtship and marriage in the text.

5. Students will identify and explain the function of dramatic and verbal irony.

6. Students will practice oral reading.

7. Students will analyze the use of epigrams in the play.

8. Students will demonstrate their creative writing skills.

9. Students will effectively inform, persuade, and express their personal opinions through their writing.

10. Students will demonstrate their understanding of the text on four levels: factual, interpretive, critical, and personal.

11. Students will make connections with the material in the text and apply the lessons learned to their lives.

12. Students will answer questions to demonstrate their knowledge and understanding of the main events and characters as they relate to the author's theme development.

13. Students will enrich their vocabularies and improve their understanding of the play through the vocabulary lessons prepared for use in conjunction with it.

14. Students will participate in large and small group discussions.

READING ASSIGNMENTS - *The Importance of Being Earnest*

Date Assigned	Assignment	Completion Date
	Reading Assignment 1 Act I	
	Reading Assignment 2 Act II	
	Reading Assignment 3 Act III	
	Whole Play Whole Play	

UNIT OUTLINE - *The Importance of Being Earnest*

1	2	3	4	5
Victorian Era Lecture Theme and Motif Prediction Distribution of Materials	Oscar Wilde Biography Theme and Motif Prediction (cont.) PVR: Act I	Study ?s Act I Jack and Algernon Venn Diagram Foils	Non-fiction Assignment	Writing Assignment #1: Inform PVR: Act II
6	7	8	9	10
Study ?s Act II Viewpoints of Marriage in the Play	Dramatic and Verbal Irony Cecily and Gwendolen Character Motivation	Oral Reading Assignment PVR: Act III	Study ?s Act III Character Review Project Assignments	Epigrams Group Work for Project
11	12	13	14	15
Ideal Husband Comparison Writing Group Work for Project	Writing Assignment #2: Persuade Group Work for Project	Writing Assignment #3: Personal Opinion Group Work for Project	Group Performances	Group Performances Vocabulary Review
16	17			
Unit Review	Test			

Key: P = Preview Study Questions V = Vocabulary Work R = Read

STUDY GUIDE QUESTIONS

STUDY GUIDE QUESTIONS - *The Importance of Being Earnest*

Assignment #1

Act I

1. At the beginning of the play, who is Algernon expecting a visit from, and how does he prepare for the visit?

2. What reason does Jack give for why he has come to Algernon's flat for tea?

3. Why does Algernon believe marriage proposals are unromantic?

4. Why does Algernon think Jack and Gwendolen will not marry?

5. What is the inscription on the cigarette case?

6. Why does Algernon believe that the cigarette case does not belong to Jack?

7. What is a "Bunburyist," and how was that label created?

8. Who is Cecily Cardew, and how is she connected to Jack?

9. Why did Jack create Ernest, his alter ego?

10. Why does Gwendolen say she was "far from indifferent" to Jack before she met him?

11. Why, specifically, does Gwendolen like the name Ernest?

12. Why is Gwendolen critical of Jack's marriage proposal?

13. How do Lady Bracknell's views on marriage differ from Gwendolen's?

14. When Lady Bracknell interviews Jack as a potential fiancé for her daughter, what additional information is learned about his character?

15. How did Jack come to live with Mr. Thomas Cardew and his family?

16. How does Lady Bracknell respond to Jack's story of his adoption?

17. How does Jack plan to get rid of his fictitious brother Ernest?

18. When Gwendolen returns to Algernon's flat, what does she say regarding Jack's conversation with Lady Bracknell?

19. How does Algernon acquire Jack's country address?

20. At the end of Act I, where does Algernon say he is going?

Assignment #2

Act II

1. What is Cecily's opinion of her uncle at the beginning of Act II?

2. What does Cecily wish Jack would do about his brother Ernest, and why does Miss Prism think it is a bad idea?

3. According to Cecily, what is the main difference between events that are recorded in a diary and those recorded in memory?

4. Why was Miss Prism's novel never published?

5. Who arrives when Miss Prism goes for a walk with Dr. Chasuble? Why is Cecily frightened to meet him?

6. What reason does Miss Prism give for why unmarried men lead "weaker vessels astray"?

7. Why does Jack arrive at his country house dressed in all black?

8. What favor does Jack ask of Dr. Chasuble?

9. How long does Algernon plan to stay at Jack's country house?

10. Why does Cecily keep a diary?

11. What does Cecily mean when she says that she and Ernest have been engaged for three months?

12. What does Cecily say that is similar to an idea expressed by Gwendolen in Act I?

13. Who arrives when Ernest leaves to speak to Dr. Chasuble?

14. How does Gwendolen respond when she learns that Cecily is Jack's ward?

15. What is the cause of the confusion between Gwendolen and Cecily?

16. How do Gwendolen and Cecily attempt to prove who is engaged to Ernest?

17. How do Cecily and Gwendolen show their resentment toward each other?

18. How is the conflict between Gwendolen and Cecily resolved?

19. What do Algernon and Jack do after the women leave the room?

20. What reasons do Algernon and Jack present for why the other person should not be christened Ernest?

Assignment #3

Act III

1. How do Cecily and Gwendolen come to forgive their fiancés?

2. How did Lady Bracknell discover her daughter's location? Where did Gwendolen tell her father she was going?

3. How does Lady Bracknell respond to Algernon's news of Bunbury's death?

4. What does Jack say that prompts Lady Bracknell to approve of Algernon's engagement to Cecily?

5. Why does Lady Bracknell disapprove of long engagements?

6. Why does Jack disapprove of the engagement between Algernon and Cecily? What examples does he present that justify the reason for his disapproval?

7. How does Lady Bracknell know Miss Prism? What is their history?

8. What was the unfortunate switch that Miss Prism made? What was the result?

9. Who is the baby that Miss Prism lost? How is this fact proven?

10. What is revealed to be the relationship between Algernon and Jack?

11. What is Jack's real name, and how is that fact revealed?

STUDY GUIDE QUESTIONS ANSWER KEY - *The Importance of Being Earnest*

Assignment #1

Act I

1. At the beginning of the play, who is Algernon expecting a visit from, and how does he prepare for the visit?
   Algernon is expecting his Aunt Augusta (Lady Bracknell) and his cousin Gwendolen to join him for afternoon tea. He has asked his servant to make cucumber sandwiches for the occasion.
2. What reason does Jack give for why he has come to Algernon's flat for tea?
   Jack knows that Gwendolen will be coming to tea. He is in love with her and intends to propose.
3. Why does Algernon believe marriage proposals are unromantic?
   Algernon feels that love is romantic only when it is uncertain. Once the proposal is accepted, the excitement is over. Love ceases to be uncertain and, therefore, becomes unromantic.
4. Why does Algernon think Jack and Gwendolen will not marry?
   Algernon believes that girls never marry the men with whom they flirt. According to Algernon's belief, since Gwendolen and Jack flirt frequently, they will not marry. Furthermore, Algernon refuses to give his consent to the marriage until Jack tells him who Cecily is.
5. What is the inscription on the cigarette case?
   The inscription reads, "From little Cecily, with her fondest love to her dear Uncle Jack."
6. Why does Algernon believe that the cigarette case does not belong to Jack?
   Jack has never mentioned Cecily before, and Algernon does not believe Jack is acquainted with anyone by that name. Additionally, Algernon refuses to believe Jack's story that Cecily is his aunt, especially since the person who wrote the inscription describes herself as "little" and addresses him as "Uncle Jack." Finally, Jack had Algernon convinced that his name is Ernest. Jack later explains that he goes by the name Jack in the country and Ernest in the city.
7. What is a "Bunburyist," and how was that label created?
   A Bunburyist is an individual who creates a fictitious relative or friend who requires constant care and attention. An individual may pretend to visit the friend or relative at a moment's notice, thereby having an excuse to avoid other engagements.
   The term "Bunburyist" is derived from the name of Algernon's fictitious friend, Mr. Bunbury, a sickly invalid whom Algernon visits in the country.
8. Who is Cecily Cardew, and how is she connected to Jack?
   Cecily Cardew is Jack's ward. She lives at Jack's country house with a governess, Miss Prism. Cecily's grandfather, Thomas Cardew, adopted Jack when he was a boy and, later, made Jack Cecily's legal guardian. Even though she is not related to Jack, Cecily respectfully calls him uncle.
9. Why did Jack create Ernest, his alter ego?
   Ever since Jack became Cecily's guardian, he has been forced to act morally in order to set a good example for her. However, Jack is not moral and upright by nature, and he feels that he needs to escape from home to be himself. For this reason, he has told his friends in the country that he has a younger brother named Ernest in the Albany, who is always getting into trouble. When Jack goes to "visit" Ernest, he actual goes to the city.

10. Why does Gwendolen say she was "far from indifferent" to Jack before she met him?
    Gwendolen has always wanted to love someone named Ernest, and when Algernon mentioned to her that he had a friend by that name, she thought that she was destined to fall in love with him.
11. Why, specifically, does Gwendolen like the name Ernest?
    Gwendolen says that she likes the way the name sounds; it has "a music of its own," and it "produces vibrations." The name Jack, in her opinion, has neither quality.
12. Why is Gwendolen critical of Jack's marriage proposal?
    Gwendolen thinks Jack took too long in asking the question and should have practiced proposing, just as her brother does.
13. How do Lady Bracknell's views on marriage differ from Gwendolen's?
    Lady Bracknell believes that a marriage should be arranged by a young woman's parents. The mother of the future bride should choose the most eligible bachelor to be her daughter's husband. The daughter should not be allowed to choose her husband herself.
14. When Lady Bracknell interviews Jack as a potential fiancé for her daughter, what additional information is learned about his character?
    Jack is twenty-nine years old, he smokes, and he professes to being ignorant rather than intelligent. He earns an income of between seven and eight thousand pounds a year from investments, but he also has fifteen hundred acres of land in the country. In town, Jack lives at house number 149 on Belgrave Square. He is a Liberal Unionist, and he does not know who is birth parents are.
15. How did Jack come to live with Mr. Thomas Cardew and his family?
    Mr. Thomas Cardew found Jack in a hand-bag in the cloak-room of Victoria Station. Cardew adopted Jack and made him a member of his family, giving him the surname Worthing after the name of the resort he was traveling to when he found him.
16. How does Lady Bracknell respond to Jack's story of his adoption?
    Lady Bracknell is unsympathetic toward Jack. She advises him to discover the identity of at least one parent, otherwise, she will not allow him to marry her daughter.
17. How does Jack plan to get rid of his fictitious brother Ernest?
    He will tell his friends that Ernest died in Paris from a severe chill.
18. When Gwendolen returns to Algernon's flat, what does she say regarding Jack's conversation with Lady Bracknell?
    Gwendolen resigns herself to the fact that they she and Jack never be married. She has lost all the influence she had over her mother, and she fears that Lady Bracknell will prevent them from marrying. Gwendolen says, however, that even though she will be forced to marry another man, she will always love Jack.
19. How does Algernon acquire Jack's country address?
    When Jack is giving Gwendolen his address in the country, Algernon overhears the information and writes it on his shirt cuff.
20. At the end of Act I, where does Algernon say he is going?
    Algernon says that he is going Bunburying.

Assignment #2

Act II

1. What is Cecily's opinion of her uncle at the beginning of Act II?
   Cecily thinks that Jack is a very serious person and that he does not enjoy her and Miss Prism's company. According to Cecily, "he often looks a little bored when [they] are together."
2. What does Cecily wish Jack would do about his brother Ernest, and why does Miss Prism think it is a bad idea?
   Cecily wishes that Jack would invite his brother to visit them in the country. She thinks that she and Miss Prism could have a positive influence on Ernest's life. However, Miss Prism does not believe that she and Cecily could reform Ernest. Furthermore, she is not sure that it would be right to do so. Miss Prism believes that "as a man sows so let him reap," or that people should be responsible for their actions.
3. According to Cecily, what is the main difference between events that are recorded in a diary and those recorded in memory?
   The events that are recorded in a diary are truthful and accurate; those that are recorded in memory are fictitious, just like those in novels.
4. Why was Miss Prism's novel never published?
   Miss Prism's novel was lost, and, as a result, it could not be published.
5. Who arrives when Miss Prism goes for a walk with Dr. Chasuble? Why is Cecily frightened to meet him?
   When Miss Prism and Dr. Chasuble are out, Algernon arrives, pretending to be Jack's brother Ernest. Cecily is frightened to meet him, not because of his reputed immoral behavior, but because she is afraid that he will look like everyone else.
6. What reason does Miss Prism give for why unmarried men lead "weaker vessels astray"?
   Unmarried men are very attractive and tempting to women. Married men, on the other hand, are attractive only to their wives.
7. Why does Jack arrive at his country house dressed in all black?
   Jack is dressed in black because he wants his friends in the country to believe that he is in mourning. Jack is carrying out his plan to eliminate his imaginary brother Ernest. He tells Miss Prism and Dr. Chasuble that he received a telegram the previous evening from the manager of the Grand Hotel in Paris; Ernest had died of a severe chill, and his body is going to be buried in Paris.
8. What favor does Jack ask of Dr. Chasuble?
   Jack asks Dr. Chasuble to christen him at half-past five that afternoon.
9. How long does Algernon plan to stay at Jack's country house?
   Algernon plans to stay for a week.
10. Why does Cecily keep a diary?
    Cecily keeps a diary to record her thoughts and impressions. She hopes to eventually have it published.
11. What does Cecily mean when she says that she and Ernest have been engaged for three months?
    Cecily fell in love with Ernest after hearing Jack talk about him and his bad behavior. She imagined that he proposed to her under the old tree on February 14th. She bought herself a ring from Ernest, and she started wearing a bracelet with a lover's knot that she promised to never take off. In addition, Cecily wrote letters to herself from Ernest. She broke off the imaginary engagement on March 22nd, because she believes that all serious engagements have to be broken off at least once. By the following week, however, the engagement was resumed.

12. What does Cecily say that is similar to an idea expressed by Gwendolen in Act I?
    Cecily says that she thinks she could love only a man named Ernest.
13. Who arrives when Ernest leaves to speak to Dr. Chasuble?
    Gwendolen arrives, wanting to speak to Jack.
14. How does Gwendolen respond when she learns that Cecily is Jack's ward?
    Gwendolen appears to be very fond of Cecily and is delighted to know her; however, she says that she wishes Cecily were older and less attractive. Gwendolen is a bit concerned that Cecily will tempt "Ernest" into being unfaithful.
15. What is the cause of the confusion between Gwendolen and Cecily?
    Gwendolen and Cecily are both engaged to Ernest, even though he does not exist. In reality, Gwendolen is engaged to Jack Worthing, who calls himself Ernest in the city, and Cecily is engaged to Algernon Moncrieff, who is pretending to be Jack's fictitious brother Ernest.
16. How do Gwendolen and Cecily attempt to prove who is engaged to Ernest?
    Each woman argues that her engagement is valid because it will soon be published in the local newspaper. Additionally, each has written about the proposal in her diary. Ernest's proposal to Cecily took place ten minutes prior to her conversation with Gwendolen, and his proposal to Gwendolen took place at 5:30 p.m. the previous day.
17. How do Cecily and Gwendolen show their resentment toward each other?
    Gwendolen accuses Cecily of being unfashionable. She makes the satiric remark that she has never seen a spade before, calls the country boring, and indicates that sugar and cake are both unfashionable at afternoon tea.
    Cecily attempts to expose Gwendolen as a hypocrite by pointing out that it is foolish for a person who hates crowds to live in a city. Furthermore, she intentionally gives Gwendolen tea with sugar and cake just to make her angry.
18. How is the conflict between Gwendolen and Cecily resolved?
    Cecily reveals that the man Gwendolen is engaged to is really her guardian, Jack Worthing. Gwendolen, in a similar fashion, says that Cecily's fiancé is her cousin, Algernon Moncrieff. Once the two women discover that they have been deceived, they unite and turn against the men.
19. What do Algernon and Jack do after the women leave the room?
    When Cecily and Gwendolen leave, the two men argue while eating muffins.
20. What reasons do Algernon and Jack present for why the other person should not be christened Ernest?
    Jack says that Algernon should not be christened because he has already had a christening. Algernon says that Jack should not be christened because Jack's imaginary brother Ernest apparently died from a severe chill, and a chill may be hereditary.

Assignment #3

Act III

1. How do Cecily and Gwendolen come to forgive their fiancés?
   Cecily and Gwendolen feel as though their fiancés' reasons for deceiving them are just. Algernon says that he pretended to be Ernest so that he could meet Cecily. Jack agrees that he pretended to be Ernest so he could frequently go to town and visit Gwendolen. The women also think that Jack and Algernon are making a great sacrifice to be christened that afternoon and renamed Ernest.

2. How did Lady Bracknell discover her daughter's location? Where did Gwendolen tell her father she was going?
   Lady Bracknell bribed Gwendolen's maid to tell her where Gwendolen went. Gwendolen had lied and said that she was attending a lecture by the University Extension Scheme on the Influence of a Permanent Income on Thought.
3. How does Lady Bracknell respond to Algernon's news of Bunbury's death?
   Lady Bracknell is happy that Bunbury is dead. She is glad that he finally "made up his mind at the last to some definite course of action."
4. What does Jack say that prompts Lady Bracknell to approve of Algernon's engagement to Cecily?
   Jack tells Lady Bracknell that Cecily is the daughter of Mr. Thomas Cardew. He then provides her with Cardew's three addresses. Additionally, Jack tells Lady Bracknell that the family solicitors are Messrs. Markby, Markby, and Markby, a fact that she finds satisfying. Finally, he tells her that Cecily has a hundred and thirty thousand pounds in funds.
5. Why does Lady Bracknell disapprove of long engagements?
   According to Lady Bracknell, long engagements allow the betrothed to learn about each other's character, which she views as a bad idea.
6. Why does Jack disapprove of the engagement between Algernon and Cecily? What examples does he present that justify the reason for his disapproval?
   Jack does not approve of Algernon's marriage to Cecily because he does not think Algernon has a strong moral character. Jack says that Algernon entered his home uninvited, pretending to be his brother Ernest, drank an entire bottle of wine that Jack was saving for himself, made Cecily fall in love with him, stayed to tea (even though he was not wanted), and ate all the muffins.
7. How does Lady Bracknell know Miss Prism? What is their history?
   Miss Prism used to work for Lord and Lady Bracknell. She left the house with a baby in a carriage, but never returned home. Weeks later, the carriage was found in Bayswater, but it contained the manuscript of a three-volume novel instead of the infant. Miss Prism and the baby could not be found.
8. What was the unfortunate switch that Miss Prism made? What was the result?
   Miss Prism accidentally put the baby she was watching in her hand-bag and her manuscript in the baby carriage. Miss Prism then accidentally left the hand-bag in the cloak-room of Victoria Station.
9. Who is the baby that Miss Prism lost? How is this fact proven?
   Jack is the baby whom Miss Prism lost. This fact is proven when he shows Miss Prism with the hand-bag, which she identifies as her own.
10. What is revealed to be the relationship between Algernon and Jack?
    Jack and Algernon are brothers.
11. What is Jack's real name, and how is that fact revealed?
    Jack's real name is Ernest. His father was a General, and his name could be found in the Army List. When Jack looks up the name, he discovers that his father's name was Ernest. Because Jack is the eldest son, he is named after his father.

MULTIPLE-CHOICE STUDY/QUIZ QUESTIONS - *The Importance of Being Earnest*

Assignment #1

Act I

1. At the beginning of the play, who is Algernon expecting a visit from?
   A. Lady Bracknell and Jack Worthing
   B. Lady Bracknell and Gwendolen Fairfax
   C. Cecily Cardew and Gwendolen Fairfax
   D. Jack Worthing and Cecily Cardew

2. What reason does Jack give for why he has come to Algernon's flat for tea?
   A. Jack wants to tell Algernon that his friend Bunbury is dead.
   B. Jack wants to propose to Algernon's cousin, Gwendolen.
   C. Jack wants to confront Algernon for visiting his ward, Cecily.
   D. Jack wants to persuade Algernon to stop Bunburying.

3. Why does Algernon believe marriage proposals are unromantic?
   A. Many marriage proposals are carried out like business deals.
   B. Arranged marriages take the joy out of marriage proposals.
   C. Men feel awkward expressing their feelings and often propose poorly.
   D. Love is romantic only when it is uncertain, before a proposal is accepted.

4. Why does Algernon think Gwendolen will never marry Jack?
   A. Women never marry the men with whom they flirt.
   B. Women never marry the men with whom they have mutual friends.
   C. Women never marry men they find uninteresting.
   D. Women never marry men who cannot tell a convincing lie.

5. What is the inscription on the cigarette case?
   A. "From little Gwendolen, with her fondest love to her dear Uncle Jack."
   B. "From little Gwendolen, with her fondest love to her dear Uncle Ernest."
   C. "From little Cecily, with her fondest love to her dear Uncle Ernest."
   D. "From little Cecily, with her fondest love to her dear Uncle Jack."

6. Which is NOT a reason Algernon believes the cigarette case does not belong to Jack?
   A. Jack's aunt would not refer to him as "Uncle Jack."
   B. Jack has never mentioned anyone named Cecily.
   C. Jack prefers snuff to cigarettes or cigars.
   D. Jack is known to everyone in the city as Ernest.

7. What is a "Bunburyist"?
   A. someone who frequently leaves home to visit a fictitious person
   B. a person who requires constant medical care and supervision
   C. a person who lives in both the city and the country
   D. a widower who marries a woman less than half his age

8. How is Cecily Cardew related to Jack?
   A. Cecily is Jack's ward.
   B. Cecily is Jack's aunt.
   C. Cecily is Jack's daughter.
   D. Cecily is Jack's sister.

9. Why did Jack create Ernest, his alter ego?
   A. Jack did not want Cecily to know about Gwendolen.
   B. Jack could not handle the pressure to always act morally.
   C. Jack wanted the freedom to travel to Paris on a whim.
   D. Jack wanted to escape the shallowness of city life.

10. Why does Gwendolen say she was "far from indifferent" to Jack before she met him?
    A. She started to love him when she heard about his kindness and generosity.
    B. She started to love him when she learned that his name is Ernest.
    C. She knew he was very rich and popular in high society.
    D. Algernon told her Jack would be superior to her other suitors.

11. Why does Gwendolen like the name Ernest?
    A. She had a childhood friend by that name.
    B. She likes the way the name sounds.
    C. Ernest is the name of her favorite uncle.
    D. She likes that the name Ernest means "truth."

12. Why is Gwendolen critical of Jack's marriage proposal?
    A. She knows Lady Bracknell would never approve.
    B. Jack is not in the financial situation to consider marrying.
    C. It appears that Jack has not practiced proposing.
    D. Jack knows that Gwendolen is in love with Algernon.

13. How does Lady Bracknell believe engagements should be made?
    A. A young woman should accept the proposal of the man she loves.
    B. A young woman should marry the wealthiest man she knows.
    C. A young woman's parents should choose a husband for her.
    D. A young woman's parents should buy her husband with a dowry.

14. Which is NOT information revealed about Jack through his interview with Lady Bracknell?
    A. Mr. Thomas Cardew made Jack Cecily's ward.
    B. Jack earns between seven and eight thousand pounds a year.
    C. Jack is a Liberal Unionist.
    D. Jack is twenty-nine years old.

15. How did Jack come to live with Mr. Thomas Cardew and his family?
    A. Mr. Thomas Cardew rescued Jack from the streets after his parents disowned him.
    B. Mr. Thomas Cardew adopted Jack when his parents were killed in an accident.
    C. Jack's parents could not afford to raise him and gave him up for adoption.
    D. Mr. Thomas Cardew found Jack in a hand-bag in the cloak-room at Victoria Station.

16. When Lady Bracknell learns that Jack does not have parents, she is
    A. relieved.
    B. understanding.
    C. saddened.
    D. unsympathetic.

17. How does Jack plan to get rid of his fictitious brother Ernest?
    A. He will tell his friends that Ernest died in Paris from a severe chill.
    B. He will confess to Gwendolen and Cecily that Ernest does not exist.
    C. He will say that Ernest has reformed and is no longer interesting.
    D. He will have Algernon pose as Ernest and then never return to his house again.

18. When Gwendolen returns to Algernon's flat, what does she say regarding Jack's conversation with Lady Bracknell?
    A. She has persuaded Lady Bracknell to accept their marriage.
    B. Although she will likely marry another man, she will remain devoted to Jack.
    C. She has persuaded Lady Bracknell to give them money for a honeymoon in Paris.
    D. Despite her mother's opposition to the marriage, she will marry Jack.

19. How does Algernon acquire Jack's country address?
    A. He follows Gwendolen to Jack's home in the country.
    B. He looks up Jack's address in the Court Guides.
    C. He steals one of Jack's calling cards with his address.
    D. He overhears Jack giving the address to Gwendolen.

20. At the end of the act, where does Algernon say he is going?
    A. He is going to the club.
    B. He is going to visit Cecily.
    C. He is going to visit Aunt Augusta.
    D. He is going Bunburying.

Assignment #2

Act II

1. At the beginning of Act II, Cecily says that her Uncle Jack is
   A. a reckless person.
   B. a serious person.
   C. an immoral person.
   D. a whimsical person.

2. Why does Miss Prism believe it not a good idea to try to reform bad men?
   A. Men are predestined to be who they are by the will of God.
   B. Men should sow what they reap and be responsible for their actions.
   C. Bad men amplify the virtues of those who are good by sharp contrast.
   D. Bad men make conversations more lively and interesting.

3. According to Cecily, what is the main difference between events that are recorded in a diary and those recorded in memory?
   A. The events in a diary are significant; those in memory are unimportant.
   B. The events in a diary are true; those in memory are fictitious.
   C. The events in a diary are interesting; those in memory are boring.
   D. The events in a diary are extraordinary; those in memory are commonplace.

4. Why was Miss Prism's novel never published?
   A. The publishers thought her novel was uninteresting.
   B. The publishers thought her novel was too scandalous.
   C. Her manuscript was lost before it was published.
   D. Her manuscript was destroyed by Lady Bracknell.

5. Why is Cecily frightened about meeting Ernest?
   A. She is afraid he will corrupt her with his immoral behavior.
   B. She is afraid Jack will feel as though she betrayed him.
   C. She is afraid he will look just like everyone else.
   D. She is afraid he will not think she is pretty.

6. What reason does Miss Prism give for why unmarried men lead "weaker vessels astray"?
   A. Unmarried men try to get their married friends to go out to clubs.
   B. Unmarried men are a bad influence on married men.
   C. Unmarried men are attractive to women; married men are attractive only to their wives.
   D. Married men are envious of unmarried men and are tempted to stray.

7. Why does Jack arrive at his country house dressed all in black?
   A. He has just returned from Ernest's funeral.
   B. He wants to make Ernest's death more convincing.
   C. He has just returned from Bunbury's funeral.
   D. He wants to make Bunbury's death more convincing.

8. What favor does Jack ask of Dr. Chasuble?
   A. to reveal the identities of his birth parents
   B. to marry him and Gwendolen that night
   C. to christen him
   D. to christen Algernon

9. How long does Algernon plan to stay at Jack's country house?
   A. a week
   B. two days
   C. a month
   D. two weeks

10. Why does Cecily keep a diary?
    A. Cecily likes to record her thoughts and impressions.
    B. During the Victorian era, all women kept a diary.
    C. She records events is case she needs to prove her word.
    D. She wants the family history recorded for the next generation.

11. How has Cecily been engaged to Ernest for three months?
    A. Algernon drunkenly proposed to Cecily at Jack's city house.
    B. Ernest and Cecily secretly became engaged in Paris.
    C. Cecily imagined that Ernest proposed to her three months earlier.
    D. Jack pretended to be Ernest, and wrote a letter proposing to Cecily.

12. Who arrives when Algernon leaves to speak to Dr. Chasuble?
    A. Gwendolen arrives, wanting to speak to Jack.
    B. Gwendolen's father arrives, looking for her.
    C. A bill collector has followed Algernon to the house.
    D. Lane has arrived to assist Jack.

13. What does Cecily say that is similar to an idea expressed by Gwendolen in Act I?
    A. She says that Jack is a very respectable name.
    B. She does not like to talk about the weather.
    C. She says that she is never wrong.
    D. She thinks she could love only a man named Ernest.

14. How does Gwendolen respond when she learns that Cecily is Jack's ward?
    A. Gwendolen is delighted to know her, but wishes Cecily were older and less attractive.
    B. Gwendolen is glad that she will have a female companion in the house.
    C. Gwendolen feels betrayed that Jack never told her that he had a ward.
    D. Gwendolen suspects that Cecily is Jack's younger sister.

15. What is the cause of the confusion between Gwendolen and Cecily?
    A. Gwendolen and Cecily have different opinions about what is fashionable.
    B. Gwendolen and Cecily cannot determine who is the real Ernest.
    C. Gwendolen and Cecily are both engaged to Ernest.
    D. Gwendolen and Cecily are both in love with Jack.

16. How do Gwendolen and Cecily attempt to prove who is really engaged to Ernest?
    A. They ask Ernest which one of them he is going to marry.
    B. They ask Miss Prism and Lady Bracknell who Ernest truly loves.
    C. They show each other the love letters that Ernest wrote them.
    D. They use their diaries to prove when they became engaged to Ernest.

17. How does Cecily demonstrate her resentment toward Gwendolen?
    A. Cecily flirts with Algernon while Gwendolen is in the room.
    B. Cecily drops tea cakes on Gwendolen's lap.
    C. Cecily gives Gwendolen tea with sugar and cake.
    D. Cecily refuses to offer Gwendolen tea and cakes.

18. How is the conflict between Gwendolen and Cecily resolved?
    A. They are informed that Ernest passed away from a severe chill.
    B. They decide that friendship is more important than marriage.
    C. Gwendolen decides to let her mother find her a husband.
    D. They realize that Ernest is actually two different men.

19. In Act II, what do Algernon and Jack do after the women leave the room?
    A. They go to dinner at the Empire Club.
    B. They argue with each other while eating muffins.
    C. They go to the rectory to be christened.
    D. They go to the city to visit Mr. Bunbury.

20. Why does Algernon feel that Jack should not be christened?
    A. Jack's family suffers from hereditary severe chills.
    B. Jack might have been christened when he was a child.
    C. Jack will have to reform his behavior if he is christened.
    D. Jack is an Anabaptist, and christening is against his religion.

Assignment #3

Act III

1. How do Gwendolen and Cecily come to forgive their fiancés?
   A. Dr. Chasuble lectures both girls about the importance of forgiveness.
   B. They decide that being married to Jack and Algernon is better than being unmarried.
   C. Jack and Algernon promise to take Cecily and Gwendolen to Paris.
   D. Cecily and Gwendolen feel as though their fiancés' reasons for deceiving them are just.

2. How did Lady Bracknell discover her daughter's location?
   A. She learned Gwendolen's location from Algernon.
   B. She overheard Jack giving Gwendolen his home address.
   C. She followed Gwendolen to Jack's country estate.
   D. She bribed Gwendolen's maid to tell her.

3. How does Lady Bracknell respond to Algernon's news of Bunbury's death?
   A. She worries that Bunbury's death was caused by a typhus epidemic.
   B. She is happy that Bunbury finally decided whether he wanted to live or die.
   C. She feels sorry for her nephew, who is grieving over his friend's death.
   D. She is furious that Bunbury chose to die at such an unfortunate time.

4. Which of the following is NOT something Jack says to get Lady Bracknell to approve of Algernon's marriage to Cecily?
   A. Cecily has one hundred and thirty thousand pounds in funds.
   B. Cecily's grandfather, Mr. Thomas Cardew, owned three homes.
   C. Cecily is the granddaughter of a French baroness.
   D. Cecily's family's solicitors are Messrs. Markby, Markby, and Markby.

5. Why does Lady Bracknell disapprove of long engagements?
   A. Long engagements lead to overly showy and expensive weddings.
   B. Long engagements lead to temptation and immoral behavior.
   C. Long engagements are a Continental fad that is unfashionable in London.
   D. Long engagements allow the betrothed to learn about each other's character.

6. Why does Jack disapprove of the engagement between Algernon and Cecily?
   A. Jack is aware of Algernon's enormous debt.
   B. Jack knows that Algernon is an alcoholic.
   C. Jack suspects that Algernon has a mistress in the city.
   D. Jack thinks that Algernon has an immoral character.

7. How does Lady Bracknell know Miss Prism?
   A. Miss Prism is Algernon's mother.
   B. Miss Prism was Algernon's nurse.
   C. Miss Prism is Lady Bracknell's sister.
   D. Miss Prism once worked for Lady Bracknell.

8. Where did Miss Prism accidentally leave her hand-bag with the baby?
   A. She left it in the cloak-room of Victoria Station.
   B. She left it in a train compartment.
   C. She left it on the counter of a flower shop.
   D. She left it on a bench in the park.

9. Who is the baby that Miss Prism lost?
   A. Jack
   B. Cecily
   C. Algernon
   D. Gwendolen

10. What is revealed to be the relationship between Algernon and Jack?
    A. Jack and Algernon are brothers.
    B. Jack is Algernon's uncle.
    C. Jack is Algernon's father.
    D. Jack and Algernon are cousins.

11. How is it determined that Jack's birth name is Ernest?
    A. Dr. Chasuble knows the rector who christened Jack when he was a baby.
    B. Jack was named after his father, whose name was Ernest.
    C. Lady Bracknell recorded Jack's real birth name in her diary.
    D. Jack's birth certificate is found within the pages of Miss Prism's manuscript.

ANSWER KEY: STUDY QUESTIONS - *The Importance of Being Earnest*

	1	2	3
1	B	B	D
2	B	B	D
3	D	B	B
4	A	C	C
5	D	C	D
6	C	C	D
7	A	B	D
8	A	C	A
9	B	A	A
10	B	A	A
11	B	C	B
12	C	A	
13	C	D	
14	A	A	
15	D	C	
16	D	D	
17	A	C	
18	B	D	
19	D	B	
20	D	A	

VOCABULARY WORKSHEETS

VOCABULARY ASSIGNMENT #1 - *The Importance of Being Earnest*

Part I: Using Prior Knowledge and Contextual Clues

Below are the sentences in which the vocabulary words appear in the text. Read the sentence. Use any clues you can find in the sentence combined with your prior knowledge, and write what you think the underlined words mean on the lines provided.

1. As far as the piano is concerned, <u>sentiment</u> is my forte.

   _____

2. Is marriage so <u>demoralizing</u> as that?

   _____

3. Lane's views on marriage seem somewhat <u>lax</u>.

   _____

4. The Divorce Court was specially invented for people whose memories are so curiously <u>constituted</u>.

   _____

5. Cecily, who addresses me as her uncle from motives of respect that you could not possibly appreciate, lives at my place in the country under the charge of her admirable <u>governess</u>, Miss Prism.

   _____

6. I may tell you <u>candidly</u> that the place is not in Shropshire.

   _____

7. Literary criticism is not your <u>forte</u>, my dear fellow.

   _____

8. I have invented an invaluable permanent <u>invalid</u> called Bunbury, in order that I may be able to go down into the country whenever I choose.

   _____

9. If it wasn't for Bunbury's extraordinary bad health, for instance, I wouldn't be able to dine with you at Willis's to-night, for I have been really <u>engaged</u> to Aunt Augusta for more than a week.

   _____

10. JACK: *[Sententiously.]* That, my dear young friend, is the theory that the corrupt French Drama has been propounding for the last fifty years.

   _____

11. That, my dear young friend, is the theory that the corrupt French Drama has been <u>propounding</u> for the last fifty years.

   _____

12. For heaven's sake, don't try to be <u>cynical</u>.

   _____

13. I'm sure the programme will be delightful, after a few <u>expurgations</u>.

   _____

14. And I often wish that in public, at any rate, you had been more <u>demonstrative</u>.

   _____

15. GWENDOLEN: *[Glibly.]* Ah! that is clearly a metaphysical speculation, and like most metaphysical speculations has very little reference at all to the actual facts of real life, as we know them.

   _____

16. Ah! that is clearly a <u>metaphysical</u> speculation, and like most <u>metaphysical</u> speculations has very little reference at all to the actual facts of real life, as we know them.

   _____

17. Besides, Jack is a <u>notorious</u> domesticity for John!

   _____

18. Besides, Jack is a notorious <u>domesticity</u> for John!

   _____

19. She would probably never be allowed to know the entrancing pleasure of a single moment's <u>solitude</u>.

   _____

20. Rise, sir, from this <u>semi-recumbent</u> posture. It is most indecorous.

   _____

21. Rise, sir, from this semi-recumbent posture. It is most <u>indecorous</u>.

    _____

22. While I am making these <u>inquiries</u>, you, Gwendolen, will wait for me below in the carriage.

    _____

23. The whole theory of modern education is <u>radically</u> unsound.

    _____

24. The whole theory of modern education is radically <u>unsound</u>.

    _____

25. Was he born in what the Radical papers call the purple of <u>commerce</u>, or did he rise from the ranks of the aristocracy?

    _____

26. The late Mr. Thomas Cardew, an old gentleman of a very charitable and kindly <u>disposition</u>, found me, and gave me the name of Worthing, because he happened to have a first-class ticket for Worthing in his pocket at the time.

    _____

VOCABULARY WORKSHEET ASSIGNMENT #1 (Continued) - *The Importance of Being Earnest*

Part II: Determining the Meaning

Match the vocabulary words to their dictionary definitions.

____ 1. SENTIMENT					A. completely and thoroughly

____ 2. DEMORALIZING				B. improper; unmannerly

____ 3. LAX						C. well-known for terrible reasons

____ 4. CONSTITUTED				D. a female who lives with and teaches children in a private home

____ 5. GOVERNESS					E. composed or constructed of

____ 6. CANDIDLY					F. a person's behavior and attitude

____ 7. FORTE						G. putting forth for others to consider

____ 8. INVALID					H. half-reclined; almost lying down

____ 9. ENGAGED					I. busy or occupied; having plans with someone or to do something

____ 10. SENTENTIOUSLY				J. spoken flippantly or without prior thought

____ 11. PROPOUNDING				K. loose or careless; not strict

____ 12. CYNICAL					L. abstract and philosophical

____ 13. EXPURGATIONS				M. items that are removed from a collection

____ 14. DEMONSTRATIVE				N. investigations; acts of questioning or obtaining information

____ 15. GLIBLY					O. bitter and distrustful

____ 16. METAPHYSICAL				P. self-righteously; expressing wise sayings and aphorisms

____ 17. NOTORIOUS					Q. depressing; disheartening

____ 18. DOMESTICITY				R. a strength or specialty

____ 19. SOLITUDE					S. impaired; not well-formed

____ 20. SEMI-RECUMBENT T. relating to the home or the household; in this usage, a nickname

____ 21. INDECOROUS U. truthfully and sincerely

____ 22. INQUIRIES V. relating to trade or business

____ 23. RADICALLY W. the state of being alone; seclusion

____ 24. UNSOUND X. expressive or affectionate

____ 25. COMMERCE Y. a person who is in frequently in poor health

____ 26. DISPOSITION Z. an emotion or feeling

VOCABULARY ASSIGNMENT #2 - *The Importance of Being Earnest*

Part I: Using Prior Knowledge and Contextual Clues

Below are the sentences in which the vocabulary words appear in the text. Read the sentence. Use any clues you can find in the sentence combined with your prior knowledge, and write what you think the underlined words mean on the lines provided.

1. Surely such a <u>utilitarian</u> occupation as the watering of flowers is rather Moulton's duty than yours?

   _____

2. But I don't like German. It isn't at all a <u>becoming</u> language.

   _____

3. Your guardian enjoys the best of health, and his <u>gravity</u> of demeanour is especially to be commended in one so comparatively young as he is.

   _____

4. Your guardian enjoys the best of health, and his gravity of demeanour is especially to be <u>commended</u> in one so comparatively young as he is.

   _____

5. Idle merriment and <u>triviality</u> would be out of place in his conversation.

   _____

6. I do not think that even I could produce any effect on a character that, according to his own brother's <u>admission</u> is irretrievably weak and vacillating.

   _____

7. I do not think that even I could produce any effect on a character that, according to his own brother's admission is <u>irretrievably</u> weak and vacillating.

   _____

8. I do not think that even I could produce any effect on a character that, according to his own brother's admission is irretrievably weak and <u>vacillating</u>.

   _____

9. Even these metallic problems have their <u>melodramatic</u> side.

   _____

10. I know he wants to speak to you about your emigrating...Uncle Jack is sending you to Australia.

11. ALGERNON: Well, would you mind me reforming myself this afternoon?
    CECILY: That is rather Quixotic of you. But I think you should try.

12. A misanthrope I can understand...a womanthrope, never!

13. MISS PRISM: A misanthrope I can understand...a womanthrope, never!
    CHASUBLE: *[With a scholar's shudder.]* Believe me, I do not deserve so neologistic a phrase.

14. *[CECILY goes towards JACK; he kisses her brow in a melancholy manner.]*
    CECILY: What is the matter Uncle Jack? Do look happy!

15. It is perfectly childish to be in deep mourning for a man who is actually staying for a whole week with you in your house as a guest. I call it grotesque.

16. The absence of old friends one can endure with equanimity.

17. ALGERNON: I'll be back in no time. *[Kisses her and rushes down the garden.]*
    CECILY: What an impetuous boy he is!

18. Miss Fairfax! I suppose one of the many good elderly women who are associated with Uncle Jack in some of his philanthropic work in London.

19. I believe the aristocracy are suffering very much from it just at present. It is almost an epidemic amongst them, I have been told.

20. To save my poor, innocent, trusting boy from the <u>machinations</u> of any other girl there are no lengths to which I would not go.

    _____

21. JACK: Yes, but you have been christened. That is the important thing.
    ALGERNON: Quite so. So I know my <u>constitution</u> can stand it.

    _____

22. Yes, but you said yourself that a severe chill was not <u>hereditary</u>.

    _____

VOCABULARY WORKSHEET ASSIGNMENT #2 (Continued) - *The Importance of Being Earnest*

Part II: Determining the Meaning

Match the vocabulary words to their dictionary definitions.

____ 1. UTILITARIAN   A. indecisive or wavering

____ 2. BECOMING   B. having to do with the giving of money or services to help others

____ 3. GRAVITY   C. depressing or spiritless

____ 4. COMMENDED   D. a widespread disease or illness

____ 5. TRIVIALITY   E. can be passed from an individual to his or her offspring

____ 6. ADMISSION   F. attractive or flattering

____ 7. IRRETRIEVABLY   G. leaving one's country to live in another

____ 8. VACILLATING   H. unnatural, bizarre, and hideous

____ 9. MELODRAMATIC   I. a confession or an acknowledgment

____ 10. EMIGRATING   J. an individual who hates people

____ 11. QUIXOTIC   K. praised or complimented

____ 12. MISANTHROPE   L. calmness and composure

____ 13. NEOLOGISTIC   M. schemes or tricks

____ 14. MELANCHOLY   N. a person's physical and mental well being

____ 15. GROTESQUE   O. rash and careless

____ 16. EQUANIMITY   P. dreamy, romantic, and idealistic

____ 17. IMPETUOUS   Q. overemotional and theatrical

____ 18. PHILANTHROPIC   R. something unimportant and superficial

____ 19. EPIDEMIC   S. relating to a word that has just been created

____ 20. MACHINATIONS   T. unable to be repaired or recovered

____ 21. CONSTITUTION   U. relating to usefulness instead of grace, beauty, or sophistication

____ 22. HEREDITARY   V. seriousness; coldness

VOCABULARY ASSIGNMENT #3 - *The Importance of Being Earnest*

Part I: Using Prior Knowledge and Contextual Clues

Below are the sentences in which the vocabulary words appear in the text. Read the sentence. Use any clues you can find in the sentence combined with your prior knowledge, and write what you think the underlined words mean on the lines provided.

1. They have been eating muffins. That looks like <u>repentance</u>.

   _____

2. They're looking at us. What <u>effrontery</u>!

   _____

3. Let us preserve a <u>dignified</u> silence.

   _____

4. His voice alone inspires one with absolute <u>credulity</u>.

   _____

5. Your Christian names are still an <u>insuperable</u> barrier.

   _____

6. <u>Apprised</u>, sir, of my daughter's sudden flight by her trusty maid, whose confidence I purchased by means of a small coin, I followed her at once by a luggage train.

   _____

7. I think some <u>preliminary</u> enquiry on my part would not be out of place.

   _____

8. Until yesterday I had no idea that there were any families or persons whose origin was a <u>Terminus</u>.

   _____

9. Miss Cardew's family <u>solicitors</u> are Messrs. Markby, Markby, and Markby.

   _____

10. Dear child, of course you know that Algernon has nothing but his debts to depend upon. But I do not approve of <u>mercenary</u> marriages.

    _____

11. Algernon is an extremely, I may almost say an <u>ostentatiously</u>, eligible young man. He has nothing, but he looks everything.

_____

12. *[ALGERNON and CECILY look at him in <u>indignant</u> amazement.]*
    LADY BRACKNELL: Untruthful! My nephew Algernon? Impossible! He is an Oxonian.

_____

13. This afternoon during my temporary absence in London on an important question of romance, he obtained admission to my house by means of the false <u>pretense</u> of being my brother.

_____

14. Well, it will not be very long before you are of age and free from the restraints of <u>tutelage</u>.

_____

15. *[...MISS PRISM grows pale and <u>quails</u>. She looks anxiously round as if desirous to escape.]*

_____

16. On the morning of the day you mention, a day that is forever branded on my memory, I prepared as usual to take the baby out in its <u>perambulator</u>.

_____

17. I had also with me a somewhat old, but <u>capacious</u> hand-bag in which I had intended to place the manuscript of a work of fiction that I had written during my few unoccupied hours.

_____

18. Here is the stain on the lining caused by the explosion of a <u>temperance</u> beverage, an incident that occurred at Leamington.

_____

19. Every luxury that money could buy, including christening, had been <u>lavished</u> on you by your fond and doting parents.

_____

20. Every luxury that money could buy, including christening, had been lavished on you by your fond and <u>doting</u> parents.

_____

VOCABULARY WORKSHEET ASSIGNMENT #3 (Continued) - *The Importance of Being Earnest*

Part II: Determining the Meaning

Match the vocabulary words to their dictionary definitions.

____ 1. REPENTANCE   A. done beforehand or in preparation for

____ 2. EFFRONTERY   B. honorable and distinguished

____ 3. DIGNIFIED   C. in a showy manner; extravagantly

____ 4. CREDULITY   D. disgusted or annoyed

____ 5. INSUPERABLE   E. protection or care by a guardian or tutor

____ 6. APPRISED   F. lawyers or legal advisers

____ 7. PRELIMINARY   G. an expression of regret for doing something wrong

____ 8. TERMINUS   H. to cringe with fear

____ 9. SOLICITORS   I. informed; given knowledge of

____ 10. MERCENARY   J. a deception or false claim

____ 11. OSTENTATIOUSLY   K. rudeness or shamelessness

____ 12. INDIGNANT   L. a baby carriage

____ 13. PRETENSE   M. unable to be bypassed or overlooked

____ 14. TUTELAGE   N. providing a service only for financial gain

____ 15. QUAIL   O. sobriety; abstaining from drinking alcohol

____ 16. PERAMBULATOR   P. a train or bus station

____ 17. CAPACIOUS   Q. spacious or having the ability to hold a lot

____ 18. TEMPERANCE   R. given in abundance

____ 19. LAVISHED   S. overly fond of and permissive

____ 20. DOTING   T. believability; inspiring trust and faith in an idea

VOCABULARY ANSWER KEY - *The Importance of Being Earnest*

	1	2	3
1	Z	U	G
2	Q	F	K
3	K	V	B
4	E	K	T
5	D	R	M
6	U	I	I
7	R	T	A
8	Y	A	P
9	I	Q	F
10	P	G	N
11	G	P	C
12	O	J	D
13	M	S	J
14	X	C	E
15	J	H	H
16	L	L	L
17	C	O	Q
18	T	B	O
19	W	D	R
20	H	M	S
21	B	N	
22	N	E	
23	A		
24	S		
25	V		
26	F		

DAILY LESSONS

LESSON ONE

Objectives:

1. To learn about the important political, economic, and social issues in the Victorian Era
2. To discuss the extent to which literature is the product of the time period in which it is written
3. To make predictions about what themes and motifs will be developed in the play

Activity 1:

Ask students the following preliminary discussion questions about the Victorian Era:

- What do you already know about the Victorian Era (1837-1901)? The Industrial Revolution? British Imperialism?

- To what extent do you think politics and the economy influence literature?

Then, present the lecture notes on the Victorian Era that accompany this lesson.

Activity 2:

When you have concluded the lecture, ask students to make predictions about the themes and motifs of the play based up on what was happening at the time it was written. Create a list of the students' answers on an overhead or poster board that can be displayed to the class. Keep a copy of the responses, and revisit them when your class has finished reading the play.

Activity 3:

Distribute the materials students will use in this unit. Explain in detail how students are to use these materials.

Study Guides: Students should read the study guide questions for each reading assignment prior to beginning the reading assignment to get a feeling for what events and ideas are important in the section they are about to read. After reading the section, students will (as a class or individually) answer the questions to review the important events and ideas from that section of the book. Students should keep the study guides as study materials for the unit test.

Vocabulary: Prior to reading a reading assignment, students will do vocabulary work related to the section of the book they are about to read. Following the completion of the reading of the book, there will be a vocabulary review of all the words used in the vocabulary assignments. Students should keep their vocabulary work as study materials for the unit test.

Reading Assignment Sheet: You need to fill in the reading assignment sheet to let students know by when their reading has to be completed. You can either write the assignment sheet up on a side blackboard or bulletin board, and leave it there for students to see each day, or you can make copies for each student to have. In either case, you should advise students to become very familiar with the reading assignments so they know what is expected of them.

Extra Activities Center: The Unit Resource Materials portion of this LitPlan contains crossword and word search puzzles. Make an extra activities center in your room where you will keep these materials for students to use. (Keep several copies of the puzzles on hand.) Explain to students that these materials are available for them to use when they finish reading assignments or other class work early.

Non-fiction Assignment Sheet: Explain to students that they will read at least one non-fiction piece at some time during the unit. Students will fill out a Non-fiction Assignment Sheet after completing the reading to help you evaluate their reading experiences and to help the students think about and evaluate their own reading experiences.

Books: Each school has its own rules and regulations regarding student use of school books. Advise students of the procedures that are normal for your school.

THE VICTORIAN ERA - *The Importance of Being Earnest*

The Industrial Revolution

The 19th century ushered in drastic changes to Britain's economy and international relations, creating a society that is relatively modern by today's standards. When Queen Victoria took the throne in 1837, it was in the midst of Britain's Industrial Resolution. The enclosure of land peaked in the 18th century, and small farmers were pushed off their land and driven into urban centers to find work. In the First Industrial Revolution, advances in technology, such as the spinning jenny (1764), the spinning mule (1779), in addition to James Watt's steam engine (1763), allowed textiles and other products to be mass produced, leading to the creation of mills and factories. The engines and other pieces of equipment that used coal, including the steam locomotive, led to a rise in the mining industry. The first modern railway was built in 1825, connecting Stockton and Darlington so that coal could be transported efficiently between the two areas. The first combination rail system, carrying both passengers and goods, was built in 1830, and connected Liverpool and Manchester.

The Second Industrial Revolution began in the middle of the 19th century, bringing with it more advances in technology. Oil began to be used as a fuel in addition to coal, and steel replaced iron. Additionally, James Watt's steam engine was replaced by the more efficient internal combustion engine, and many engineers, including Nikola Tesla and Thomas Edison, began experimenting with and creating uses for electricity. England was quickly becoming the Industrial epicenter of the Western world.

Life for the working class was terrible. The urban poor worked long hours in the factories and the mines, most often in unsafe conditions that could cause serious injury or death. In the beginning of the period, women and children were not exempt from doing labor-intensive work, and they even worked underground in the mines. While people worked twelve to fourteen hours a day on average, they could work as many as twenty, and at the end of a long shift, would bring a meager wage to a home that was small, filthy, and overcrowded. Entire families occupied single rooms in tenement houses. With no waste disposal, and no sewage system until 1859, the streets were filled with garbage and excrement. Smoke from the factories filled the air and covered all of the buildings with black soot. Water supplies were polluted with chemicals from the mills, and tuberculosis, cholera, and typhus were widespread.

Prostitution was also prevalent in the slums of Victorian England. While some women were courtesans, or mistresses to wealthy patrons, most were single, poor women who either unemployed or needed an additional income to support themselves and their children. Although prostitution was illegal, and religious organizations constantly strove to eliminate the practice, it was relatively common for men, even those in the upper echelons of society, to hire prostitutes and purge themselves of the excess sexual energy that Victorian scientists believed was part of their biological makeup.

However, life for the working classes improved with several labor reforms passed during Victoria's reign. Children under nine and women were prohibited from working in the mines; workdays were limited to ten hours or less.

The Creation of the Middle Class and the "Cult of Domesticity"

The 19th century and the Victorian Era also saw the rise of the middle class, men who earned money through industry and commerce, becoming wealthy bankers, businessmen, and factory owners. Because their wealth equaled—sometimes even surpassed—that of the old, landed elite, they were deprecated by the upper class. The middle class, on the other hand, viewed the aristocrats with disdain, scorning their relaxed, carefree, lazy lifestyles that were in opposition to utility and usefulness, which the middle class valued above all else.

The new middle class gave rise to the "Cult of Domesticity" and "gender spheres," which contributed to the strict moral code associated with the Victorian Era. Rather than marrying for money and estates like the landed elite, members of the middle class married those they respected and knew could share the responsibilities. While men occupied the "public sphere," engaging in commerce and business transactions, women occupied the "private sphere," doing household chores, raising the children, and, on occasion, helping with some aspects of the business.

In addition to their other duties, women were put in charge of the moral education and wellbeing of their families. In the Victorian Era, it was believed that women were not as passionate as men were and that their sexual appetites were not as great. For this reason, they were believed to be innately moral and good. Even discrete suggestions of sex could offend their delicate sensibilities, and for this reason, extreme measures were taken to avoid even the most indirect hints of sexuality.

British Imperialism

The Victorian Era also coincided with the age of British Imperialism, which was largely caused by the Industrial Revolution. Since Britain had become a big industrial and commercial center, it needed to acquire new territory and rely on existing colonies for its supply of raw materials. Farms in Eastern Europe supplied the country with most of its wheat and grain; cotton was grown in the United States; sugar came from the Caribbean. Additionally, Britain expanded into India for its rubber, opium, spices, and silks, then, went to southern and eastern Africa for gold and diamonds. Additionally, Britain needed to find new markets for its goods, hence why it entered the Crimean War to defend its trade routes and struggled to maintain trade in the Chinese port city of Canton, resulting in the Opium Wars. Expansion allowed Britain to sell the goods and purchase the exotic wares that the upper-middle class desired.

There were also social and ideological reasons behind British Imperialism. Charles Darwin's book, On the Origin of Species (1859), introduced the ideas of natural selection and evolution, which, in turn, changed the way some people viewed race and culture. Just as natural selection limits populations in the animal world, allowing the strong individuals to survive and the weak to perish, it also allowed some races and civilizations to prevail over others. It was believed that the British—with their industry, their international trade, and their advances in science and technology—were superior to the indigenous people of Africa and India. Those who were sympathetic toward the native people in the new territories felt that it was their duty, the "white man's burden" to civilize the people. Travel journals and reports of Africa and the East both fascinated and disturbed the British people. Tales about the Sati, harem women, pleasure domes, opium dens, and strange barbaric customs led many to believe that the Africans and Easterners were heathens who could be saved only through Christianity. Thus, the British travelers to the East were not only of adventurers seeking a fortune, but missionaries who wanted the natives to abandon their heathen traditions and join the Anglican Church.

Needless to say, this created a clash of cultures that developed into a few rebellions and wars. The following are some of the most significant:

Opium Wars – In the 19th century, the British desired the silk, porcelain, and tea that China produced; however, in China, European goods were not in demand, and the Chinese accepted only silver as payment. However, when the British government outlawed the export of gold and silver, merchants began to sell another commodity to the Chinese: opium, which was readily produced in British-occupied India. When the Daoguang Emperor outlawed opium, and the British continued trafficking it in Canton, China's major trading port with the West, hostilities arose leading to the First Opium War (1839-1842), and after the subsequent treaty, the Treaty of Nanjing, was broken, the Second Opium War (1852-1860). As a result of Britain's victories, ten new port cities were opened in China. Western missionaries and merchants were permitted to enter the country, and China had to pay three million ounces of silver to Britain as reparation.

The Indian Rebellion of 1857 – The British East India Company—an English joint-stock company with military power—had been in India since 1757, and by the Victorian Era, there was great tension between the British and the Indians. The company stripped Indian princes and nobles of their land, cut the pay of the natives in their surface, and even though it was against company practice, attempted to convert the Indian soldiers and workers to Christianity.

However, the biggest conflict developed in 1857, with the introduction of the Pattern 1853 Enfield Musket. Rumors circulated that the cartridges, which had to be bitten open, were greased with beef tallow or pig fat. The Muslim and Hindu soldiers in the British army, also known as sepoys, were prohibited from consuming beef and pork products because of their religion. The soldiers who refused to bite the cartridges and were arrested for insubordination, and in May 1857, sepoys who were awaiting sentencing in Meerut turned against their officers. Other mutinies and rebellions started in the country, and it took the British a year to get India back under its control. In 1858, the British East India Company was dissolved. India came under the direct control of the British Empire, and Queen Victoria declared herself Empress of India.

Crimean War – After debating who had the most authority in the Holy Land, France or Russia, Sultan Abdülmecid I decided in favor of France. Tsar Nicholas I of Russia responded by sending troops into the Danubian Principalities in July 1853. When peace negations failed, Turkey declared war on Russia. The British, who feared Russian imperial expansion and wanted to protect their trade routes in the Mediterranean, entered the war in support of the Ottomans and France. A series of battles ensued and eventually concluded with the Treaty of Paris. Russia neutralized the Black Sea region, the ports to merchants of all countries and Moldavia and Wallachia became independent states. Today, the Crimean War is considered the first modern war due to its use of telegraphs and railways. Additionally, it was the war in which the famous Florence Nightingale and her staff cared for the British soldiers who were wounded in battle.

Aestheticism and the Dandy

The Aesthetic Movement (called the Decadence Movement in France) is derived from a phrase allegedly coined by philosopher Vincent Cousin in 1818, and later developed by Théophile Gautier: l'art pour l'art or "art for art's sake." The aesthetes believed that art's purpose is to be beautiful and evoke feelings of sensual pleasure; one should not assess art based upon its usefulness or the moral it conveys. As Oscar Wilde says in his Preface to The Picture of Dorian Gray, "There is no such thing as a moral or an immoral book. Books are well written, or badly written…We can forgive a man for making a useful thing as long as he does not admire it. The only excuse for making a useless thing is that one admires it intensely. All art is quite useless."

The Aesthetic Movement was not restricted to art and literature; it also encompassed furniture, home décor, and fashion. The dandy is a product of both the Aesthetic Movement's impact on 19th-century fashion and the backlash against Victorian morals. Initially, a dandy was a person of the middle class who, as a form of protest against the rigid class system, imitated the aristocratic style of dress. However, by the late 1800s, the style ceased to be a political statement and evolved into something different. A dandy was an individual who shunned the ideas of utility and usefulness, and instead, lived for the pursuit of pleasure and recreation. He dressed extravagantly, displaying his wealth in expensive clothing, and instead of working, spent most of his day involved in leisure activities. Additionally, while the dandy revolted against the strict morals of the Victorian Era, he held proper etiquette and speech in high regard. Just as the Aesthetic Movement stressed the importance of beauty and sensuality in art, the dandy did in life.

LESSON TWO

Objectives:

1. To learn about Oscar Wilde's life
2. To continue to make predictions about the themes and motifs in the play
3. To discuss opinions on topics that will appear in the play

Activity 1:

Copy and distribute the information about Oscar Wilde's life in the About the Author section of this LitPlan, or read the information aloud to your students.

Have students revise the list of themes and motifs they believe will be present in the play based on what they have learned about Oscar Wilde. Keep a copy of your students' list so that you can return to it when the class has finished reading the play.

Activity 2:

Have students preview the study questions for Act I, complete the vocabulary worksheet for that section, and perform a close reading of the act before the next class meeting.

LESSON THREE

Objectives:

1. To demonstrate reading comprehension through sharing responses to the study guide questions
2. To analyze the characters of Jack and Algernon by viewing them as foils

Activity 1:

Give students a few minutes to formulate answers for the Act I study guide questions. You could have students answer the questions individually, in pairs, or in small groups. When your students have finished, have them share their responses with the class and correct any mistakes they made. Allow them to keep the questions for study purposes.

Activity 2:

Copy and distribute the Comparing and Contrasting Jack & Algernon worksheet. Have each student re-read Act I of the play, and complete the Venn Diagram on the worksheet. In particular, ask your students to comment on the following:

Social Identity: To what social class does each character belong? With whom does he associate? In what kinds of activities does the character engage?

Values and Beliefs: What ideas and opinions does each character hold? What does he value? What are his ideas concerning morality? Does he conform to the social norm?

Speech and Behavior: How does the character speak? Is he respectful or disrespectful to the other characters? Are his speeches carefully planned, or does he speak recklessly? How does he use language? Is he serious or lighthearted?

General Characteristics: What are some qualities and traits that the character possesses?

Activity 3:

Present the following definition of foil to the class: A foil is a character whose qualities or actions usually serve to emphasize the actions or qualities of the main character, the protagonist, by providing a strong contrast.

Have the students, using the information in their completed Venn Diagrams, determine how Algernon and Jack serve as foils to each other. It may help them to make a list of how Algernon, as a contrast to Jack, helps emphasize aspects of Jack's character and vice versa.

When they finish, have students share their answers with the class.

COMPARING AND CONTRASTING JACK & ALGERNON - *The Importance of Being Earnest*

Directions: Complete the following Venn Diagram for Jack & Algernon. In particular, comment on *social identity, values and beliefs, speech and behavior* and *general characteristics*.

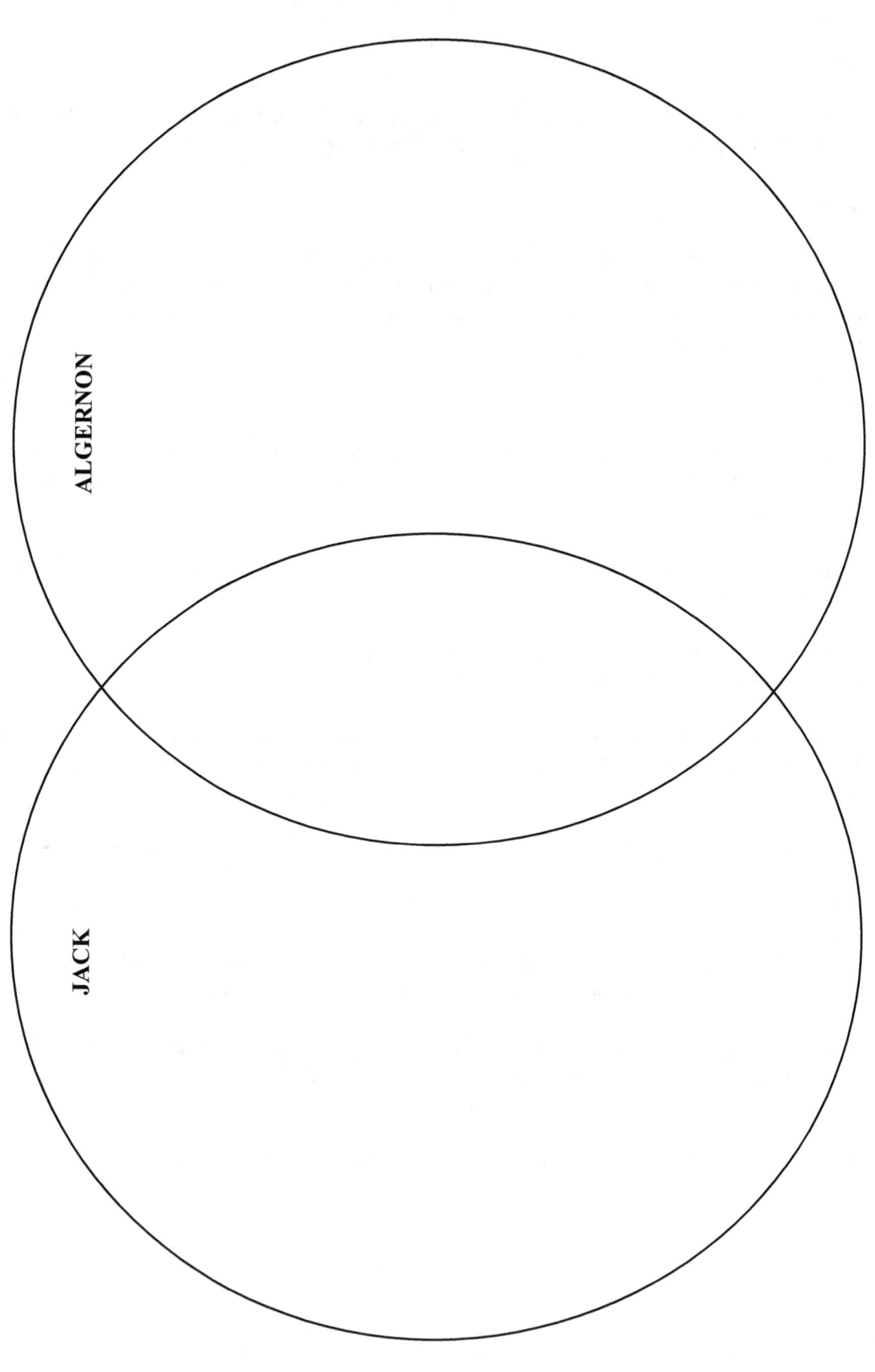

LESSON FOUR

Objectives:

1. To broaden students' knowledge about topics related to the play
2. To have students research and read non-fiction related to the play to help connect the play to history

Activity 1:

Distribute the Non-fiction Assignment Sheet to students. Explain that they should choose a nonfiction topic related to *The Importance of Being Earnest*, and read a substantial article related to that topic. Then, complete the Non-fiction Assignment Sheet for that article. Students may use magazines, newspapers, and the Internet as sources.

You could suggest that your students research upper-class marriage conventions in Victorian England; Writing Assignment #1 will be about this issue.

Activity 2:

Have students read Act II of *The Importance of Being Earnest* out loud in class. You probably know the best way to choose readers for your class: pick students at random, ask for volunteers, or use whatever method works best for your students. If you have not yet completed an oral reading evaluation for your students this marking period, this would be a good opportunity to do so. A form is included with this unit for your convenience.

If students do not complete reading Act II in class, they should do so prior to the next class meeting.

NON-FICTION ASSIGNMENT SHEET - *The Importance of Being Earnest*

(To be completed after reading the required nonfiction article)

Name: _____ Date: _____

Title of Non-fiction Read: _____

Author: _____ Date Published: _____

I. Factual Summary

Write a short summary of the work you read.

II. Vocabulary

1. Which vocabulary words were difficult to understand to some degree?

2. How did you resolve your lack of understanding of these words?

III. Interpretation

What was the main point the author wanted you to get from reading his or her work?

IV. Criticism

1. Which points did you agree with or find easy to accept? Why?

2. Which points did you disagree with or find difficult to believe? Why?

V. Personal Response

What do you think about this work? OR, How does this work influence your ideas?

ORAL READING EVALUATION FORM - *The Importance of Being Earnest*

Name: _____ Class: _____ Date: _____

SKILL	EXCELLENT	GOOD	AVERAGE	FAIR	POOR
Fluency	5	4	3	2	1
Clarity	5	4	3	2	1
Audibility	5	4	3	2	1
Pronunciation	5	4	3	2	1
_____	5	4	3	2	1
_____	5	4	3	2	1

Total: _____ Grade: _____

Comments:

_____
_____
_____
_____
_____
_____
_____
_____
_____
_____

LESSON FIVE

Objectives:

1. To research upper-class marriage conventions in Victorian England
2. To have students write an informational essay based on the information they find

Activity 1:

Copy and distribute Writing Assignment #1 (Informational) about the upper-class courtship and marriage conventions in the Victorian Era. Take students to the library/media center where they can begin their research in preparation for this assignment.

Activity 2:

Have students preview the study questions for Act II, complete the vocabulary worksheet for that section, and perform a close reading of the act before the next class meeting.

WRITING ASSIGNMENT #1 - *The Importance of Being Earnest*

Informational: Courtship & Marriage in the Victorian Era

Prompt:

The Importance of Being Earnest focuses not only on issues of mistaken identity, but also on courtship and marriage in the Victorian Era. The motif first presents itself in Act I, when Jack proposes to Gwendolen, and Lady Bracknell expresses disapproval of the match. The reader can correctly assume that this play is a romantic comedy and that ideas of love, engagement, and marriage will be prevalent.

Research the conventions of upper-class courtship and marriage in the Victorian Era, answering the following questions:

- Why was marriage important in the Victorian Era?
- In general, at what age did men and women get married?
- What characteristics did men and women typically look for in their marriage partners?
- Where and how did people interested in marriage initially meet?
- How did two people who were interested in each other become better acquainted?
- How did men and women become engaged?
- How much involvement did the fiancés' families have in their engagement and marriage?

Pre-writing:

After researching the required information at the library/media center, use your findings to write a report about Victorian upper-class courtship and marriage. Paraphrase or summarize what you have read instead of using direct quotations.

Drafting:

Introduce your topic in the first paragraph, being sure to end it with a thesis statement. Then, write several body paragraphs, each describing the courtship and marriage conventions in Victorian society. Conclude your essay by making modern connections to the courtship and marriage practices in the 21st century.

Peer Conference/Revising:

When you finish the rough draft of your composition, ask a student who sits near you to read it. After reading your draft, your classmate should tell you what he or she liked best about your work, which parts were difficult to understand, and ways in which your work could be improved. Reread your paper considering your classmate's comments, and make the corrections you think are necessary.

Proofreading/Editing:

Do a final proofreading of your essay, double-checking your grammar, spelling, organization, and the clarity of your ideas.

WRITING EVALUATION FORM - *The Importance of Being Earnest*

Name: _____ Date: _____ Writing Assignment # ____

Grade: _____

Circle One For Each Item:

Grammar:	excellent	good	fair	poor
Spelling:	excellent	good	fair	poor
Punctuation:	excellent	good	fair	poor
Legibility:	excellent	good	fair	poor
_____ :	excellent	good	fair	poor
_____ :	excellent	good	fair	poor

Strengths:

_____
_____
_____
_____
_____
_____

Weaknesses:

_____
_____
_____
_____
_____
_____

Comments/Suggestions:

_____
_____
_____
_____
_____
_____

LESSON SIX

Objectives:

1. To demonstrate reading comprehension through sharing responses to the study guide questions
2. To perform a close reading of the text to determine how various characters view love and marriage
3. To determine whether the viewpoints expressed by the characters conform to Victorian marriage conventions, intentionally deviate from them, or are satirical representations
4. To compare Victorian courtship and marriage conventions to those of the 21st century

Activity 1:

Give students a few minutes to formulate answers for the Act II study guide questions. You could have students answer the questions individually, in pairs, or in small groups. When your students have finished, have them share their responses with the class and correct any mistakes they made. Allow them to keep the questions for study purposes.

Activity 2:

Have your students analyze the different views of love and marriage presented in Acts I and II. On a separate sheet of paper, have them write down the opinions expressed by the following characters:

- Lane
- Algernon
- Gwendolen
- Lady Bracknell
- Miss Prism
- Cecily

When students have finished, have them answer the following questions:

1. Which of the viewpoints expressed, if any, appear to conform to the social norms of the Victorian Era?

2. Are any of the opinions expressed consistent with any trends that were becoming prevalent in the Victorian Era?

3. Are any of the opinions expressed satires of late 19th-century views of love and marriage?

LESSON SEVEN

Objectives:

1. To learn to identify verbal and dramatic irony, and explain how both function in the play
2. To analyze the conflict and character motivations of Cecily and Gwendolen

Activity 1:

Present the definitions of the following two types of irony to your class:

- *Dramatic irony* – Dramatic irony occurs when the words or actions of a character reveal his or her ignorance toward a particular situation, while the reader correctly understands the situation.

- *Verbal irony* – Verbal irony occurs when a writer, speaker, or narrator uses words to say one thing when he or she really means the opposite. One popular form of verbal irony is sarcasm.

Have students find at least three examples of each type of irony in Act II, and explain what each example lends to the play (i.e., Does the irony help develop the character? Does it help raise suspense?) While there are several examples of dramatic and verbal irony in Act II, you could allow students to find examples in Act I as well.

Activity 2:

Have your students re-read the section of Act II in which Gwendolen and Cecily first meet, beginning with Cecily's line, "Pray let me introduce myself to you," and ending with her line, "No, men are so cowardly, aren't they?"

Then, have students imagine they are directing a production of *The Importance of Being Earnest*, and the actresses playing Gwendolen and Cecily are having difficulty portraying the characters in this scene. Have students, working individually, write a paragraph or two for each character addressing the following issues:

- how the character's traits and background would affect her speech and behavior

- what the character knows about the Ernest deception, and how her limited knowledge would affect her viewpoint

- what the character knows about the other woman

- how the character interprets the other woman's involvement with Ernest

- how the character would feel about the situation

- how the character would like the other woman to think she feels

Students may use information from Act I to complete this assignment, but they should not read ahead to Act III.

LESSON EIGHT

Objectives:

1. To evaluate students' oral reading

Activity 1:

Have students read Act III of *The Importance of Being Earnest* out loud in class. You probably know the best way to choose readers for your class: pick students at random, ask for volunteers, or use whatever method works best for your students. If you have not yet completed an oral reading evaluation for your students, this would be a good opportunity to do so. A form is included with this unit for your convenience.

Activity 2:

Have students preview the study questions for Act III, complete the vocabulary worksheet for that section, and finish reading the play if they have not done so already.

LESSON NINE

Objectives:

1. To demonstrate reading comprehension through sharing responses to the study guide questions
2. To review the characters in the play, create visual depictions of them, and determine how they are interconnected
3. To have students begin working on their group projects

Activity 1:

Give students a few minutes to formulate answers for the Act III study guide questions. You could have students answer the questions individually, in pairs, or in small groups. When your students have finished, have them share their responses with the class and correct any mistakes they made. Allow them to keep the questions for study purposes.

Activity 2:

In Act III, the mystery of Jack's parentage is finally solved, and previously unknown relationships between the characters are revealed. For instance, the story of the hand-bag reveals that Jack and Algernon are brothers, which consequently, would make Jack Lady Bracknell's nephew and Gwendolen's cousin.

Have students create an intricate character web on a piece of poster board by doing the following:

- writing each character's name and a short biography of him or her

- including a portrait, either drawn or printed from the Internet, that represents each character

- drawing a dotted line between the characters and indicating how they are related or how they became acquainted

- a few quotes by each character that helps define him or her and his or her manner of speech

Students could complete this activity individually or in small groups.

Activity 3:

Copy and distribute the Project: Rewriting and Acting a Scene worksheet. Then, divide the class into groups. Six groups containing the exact number of people as characters in the scene would be ideal; however, this is not necessary.

Go over the instructions with your students, answering any questions they may have. Performances should be scheduled at least a week and a half after the assignment date. While the assignment has students perform their rewritten scenes in front of the class, students could also record their performances outside of class using a video camera.

Also accompanying this activity is an evaluation sheet that can be used for grading the performances.

PROJECT: REWRITING AND ACTING A SCENE - *The Importance of Being Earnest*

Choose from one of the following scenes in the play:

Act I: Algernon's Conversation with Jack

- **Beginning:** ALGERNON: Did you hear what I was playing, Lane?
- **Ending:** ALGERNON: Yes, but you must be serious about it…
- **Characters:** Jack, Algernon, and Lane

Act I: Aunt Augusta's Arrival and Jack's Proposal to Gwendolen

- **Beginning:** LANE: Lady Bracknell and Miss Fairfax.
- **Ending:** CURTAIN
- **Characters:** Jack, Algernon, Lane, Lady Bracknell, and Gwendolen

Act II: Ernest's Arrival at the Manor House

- **Beginning:** MISS PRISM: [Calling.] Cecily, Cecily!...
- **Ending:** CECILY: What an impetuous boy he is!...
- **Characters:** Miss Prism, Cecily, Chasuble, Merriman, Algernon, Jack

Act II: Cecily and Gwendolen Meet

- **Beginning:** MERRIMAN: A Miss Fairfax has just called to see Mr. Worthing….
- **Ending:** CURTAIN
- **Characters:** Merriman, Cecily, Gwendolen, Algernon, Jack

Act III: Reconciliation and Solving the Mystery of Jack's Birth

(ENTIRE ACT)

- **Characters:** Gwendolen, Cecily, Algernon, Jack, Lady Bracknell, Miss Prism, Chasuble

Rewrite the scene as if it were taking place in present day. Follow these guidelines:

While each of the primary characters (i.e., Jack, Algernon, Gwendolen, Cecily, and Lady Bracknell) may speak differently and use colloquial speech, his or her essence must remain the same. For example, Algernon must be witty and careless; Cecily must be romantic and naïve. However, there are a few exceptions:

- The gender of the characters may be changed to reflect the people in the group; however, an actor may play a character of the opposite gender if he or she chooses to.

- Minor characters (i.e., Merriman, Miss Prism, Canon Chasuble, and Lane) may be cut from the scene or given larger roles depending on the size of the group. Actors may play more than one part if necessary, but all members of the group must have speaking roles.

- If there are more people in the group than characters in the scene, you may add additional characters.

- The basic idea of the scene and the important plot developments it contains must be present in the new version.

- The length of the rewritten scene must be approximately the same length as the original.

- While all characters should wear modern clothing, actors must be in costume. The costumes should allow the audience to identify they characters even before they present their lines.

- At least three props must be used in the scene. Additionally, there must be scenery of some kind.

- All lines must be rehearsed, and your teacher must have a copy of your script.

GROUP PRESENTATION EVALUATION SHEET - *The Importance of Being Earnest*

Each of the following areas should be graded on a scale of 1-5; 1 designates poor work, but a 0 can be given for absolutely no participation. The total score should be multiplied by 5 to get the final grade (out of 100%).

- Part I: individual contribution during the preparation stage
- Part II: individual contribution to the final performance
- Part III: the group's adherence to the project guidelines
- Part IV: the group's incorporation of new, creative elements

Student Name	Part I	Part II	Part III	Part IV	Total Score

LESSON TEN

Objectives:

1. To identify and analyze epigrams in the play
2. To have students begin studying for the test by identifying and explaining important quotes from the play
3. To have students begin brainstorming ideas for their group projects

Activity 1:

Introduce students to epigrams by presenting the following definition: An epigram is a witty short statement or poem that makes a general comment about life.

If students require an example of an epigram, it might help to give them this one from Oscar Wilde's The Picture of Dorian Gray: "[T]here is only one thing in the world worse than being talked about, and that is not being talked about." The epigram is witty and humorous, but it does have a somewhat profound meaning: it is better to be infamous than ignored.

Have the students skim through *The Importance of Being Earnest*, and find five epigrams in the play. On a note card, have them write the quote on one side and then on the reverse, the following information:

- the speaker
- the context of the quote
- the meaning

When they have finished, have your class divide into pairs. Students can quiz each other by identifying the epigrams.

Activity 2:

Have your class divide into their project groups and begin brainstorming ideas for their presentations. If they need help getting started, you could have them answer the following questions:

1. What are the main plot developments that need to be addressed in your scene? Would they still be relevant in today's time period, or would they need to be altered in some way to appeal to a modern audience?

2. How can the scene be rewritten in a way that would allow all members of your group to have speaking roles, without taking away from the essence of the play?

3. How will your characters dress? How will you design the scenery? How will you incorporate props into your scene?

4. What new, creative elements can you put into your scene to make it original and fun?

LESSON ELEVEN

Objectives:

1. To read Act I of *An Ideal Husband* to determine Oscar Wilde's style

Activity 1:

Copy and distribute the ANALYZING OSCAR WILDE'S STYLE chart. If you do not have copies of Wilde's *An Ideal Husband* in your classroom, copy and distribute Act I of the play, which accompanies this LitPlan. To save paper, you could have your students read Act I online at any website that contains text in the public domain. Additionally, you may divide the class into small groups, have them share the photocopied act, and work on the assignment together.

Before reading Act I of *An Ideal Husband*, have your students write down the primary literary, thematic, and plot devices found in *The Importance of Being Earnest*. If they are having difficulty getting started, you may suggest Wilde's use of epigrams, which they identified and analyzed in a previous activity. Students should record their answers in the first column of the chart.

When the class has finished the first part of the activity, have students read Act I of *An Ideal Husband*, recording literary, thematic, and plot devices just as they had for the other play. Then, have them underline or highlight devices that are found in both plays.

Finally, reconvene the class, and have groups share their answers to the following question: How would you describe Oscar Wilde's style?

Activity 2:

Divide the class into groups, and have students resume working on their presentations. At this point, groups should have the majority, if not all, of their planning done and should be writing their scenes.

Students may initially find it difficult to write the script as a group. To avoid having one or two students doing the majority of the work, you could have the group write the script together from beginning to end, but each student could supply the lines of the character he or she is playing. The script can be revised later to ensure the cohesion of the scene.

It may help students to keep the following questions in mind when writing their characters' lines:

- What is the overall message that character wants to express?
- What is the character's tone?
- How would the characters speak if he or she were living in the 21st century?

ANALYZING OSCAR WILDE'S STYLE - *The Importance of Being Earnest*

Directions: After reading Act I of *An Ideal Husband*, use the chart below to help identify Wilde's unique style and voice. Look for some prominent literary, thematic, and plot devices that Wilde uses in each plays. When you have finished, highlight or underline devices that are used in both *An Ideal Husband* and *The Importance of Being Earnest*.

The Importance of Being Earnest	*An Ideal Husband*

AN IDEAL HUSBAND - The Importance of Being Earnest

by Oscar Wilde

Act I

The octagon room at Sir Robert Chiltern's house in Grosvenor Square.

[The room is brilliantly lighted and full of guests. At the top of the staircase stands LADY CHILTERN, a woman of grave Greek beauty, about twenty-seven years of age. She receives the guests as they come up. Over the well of the staircase hangs a great chandelier with wax lights, which illumine a large eighteenth-century French tapestry—representing the Triumph of Love, from a design by Boucher—that is stretched on the staircase wall. On the right is the entrance to the music-room. The sound of a string quartette is faintly heard. The entrance on the left leads to other reception rooms. MRS. MARCHMONT and LADY BASILDON, two very pretty women, are seated together on a Louis Seize sofa. They are types of exquisite fragility. Their affectation of manner has a delicate charm. Watteau would have loved to paint them.]

MRS. MARCHMONT
Going on to the Hartlocks' tonight, Margaret? LADY BASILDON I suppose so. Are you?

MRS. MARCHMONT
Yes. Horribly tedious parties they give, don't they?

LADY BASILDON
Horribly tedious! Never know why I go. Never know why I go anywhere.

MRS. MARCHMONT
I come here to be educated.

LADY BASILDON
Ah! I hate being educated!

MRS. MARCHMONT
So do I. It puts one almost on a level with the commercial classes, doesn't it? But dear Gertrude Chiltern is always telling me that I should have some serious purpose in life. So I come here to try to find one.

LADY BASILDON
[Looking round through her lorgnette.] I don't see anybody here tonight whom one could possibly call a serious purpose. The man who took me in to dinner talked to me about his wife the whole time.

MRS. MARCHMONT
How very trivial of him!

LADY BASILDON
Terribly trivial! What did your man talk about?

MRS. MARCHMONT
About myself.

LADY BASILDON
[Languidly.] And were you interested?

MRS. MARCHMONT
[Shaking her head.] Not in the smallest degree.

LADY BASILDON
What martyrs we are, dear Margaret!

MRS. MARCHMONT
[Rising.] And how well it becomes us, Olivia!

[They rise and go towards the music room. The VICOMTE DE NANJAC, a young attaché known for his neckties and his Anglomania, approaches with a low bow, and enters into conversation.]

MASON
[Announcing guests from the top of the staircase.] Mr. and Lady Jane Barford. Lord Caversham.

[Enter LORD CAVERSHAM, an old gentleman of seventy, wearing the riband and star of the Garter. A fine Whig type. Rather like a portrait by Lawrence.]

LORD CAVERSHAM
Good evening, Lady Chiltern! Has my good-for-nothing young son been here?

LADY CHILTERN
[Smiling.] I don't think Lord Goring has arrived yet.

MABEL CHILTERN
[Coming up to LORD CAVERSHAM.] Why do you call Lord Goring good-for-nothing?

[MABEL CHILTERN is a perfect example of the English type of prettiness, the apple-blossom type. She has all the fragrance and freedom of a flower. There is ripple after ripple of sunlight in her hair, and the little mouth, with its parted lips, is expectant, like the mouth of a

child. She has the fascinating tyranny of youth, and the astonishing courage of innocence. To sane people she is not reminiscent of any work of art. But she is really like a Tanagra statuette, and would be rather annoyed if she were told so.]

LORD CAVERSHAM
Because he leads such an idle life.

MABEL CHILTERN How can you say such a thing? Why, he rides in the Row at ten o'clock in the morning, goes to the Opera three times a week, changes his clothes at least five times a day, and dines out every night of the season. You don't call that leading an idle life, do you?

LORD CAVERSHAM
[Looking at her with a kindly twinkle in his eyes.] You are a very charming young lady!

MABEL CHILTERN
How sweet of you to say that, Lord Caversham! Do come to us more often. You know we are always at home on Wednesdays, and you look so well with your star!

LORD CAVERSHAM
Never go anywhere now. Sick of London Society. Shouldn't mind being introduced to my own tailor; he always votes on the right side. But object strongly to being sent down to dinner with my wife's milliner. Never could stand Lady Caversham's bonnets.

MABEL CHILTERN
Oh, I love London Society! I think it has immensely improved. It is entirely composed now of beautiful idiots and brilliant lunatics. Just what Society should be.

LORD CAVERSHAM
Hum! Which is Goring? Beautiful idiot, or the other thing?

MABEL CHILTERN
[Gravely.] I have been obliged for the present to put Lord Goring into a class quite by himself. But he is developing charmingly!

LORD CAVERSHAM Into what?

MABEL CHILTERN
[With a little curtsey.] I hope to let you know very soon, Lord Caversham!

MASON
[Announcing guests.] Lady Markby. Mrs. Cheveley.

[Enter LADY MARKBY and MRS. CHEVELEY. LADY MARKBY is a pleasant, kindly, popular woman, with gray hair a la marquise and good lace. MRS. CHEVELEY, who accompanies her, is tall and rather slight. Lips very thin and highly coloured, a line of scarlet on a pallid face. Venetian red hair, aquiline nose, and long throat. Rouge accentuates the natural paleness of her complexion. Gray-green eyes that move restlessly. She is in heliotrope, with diamonds. She looks rather like an orchid, and makes great demands on one's curiosity. In all her movements she is extremely graceful. A work of art, on the whole, but showing the influence of too many schools.]

LADY MARKBY
Good evening, dear Gertrude! So kind of you to let me bring my friend, Mrs. Cheveley. Two such charming women should know each other!

LADY CHILTERN
[Advances towards MRS. CHEVELEY with a sweet smile. Then suddenly stops, and bows rather distantly.] I think Mrs. Cheveley and I have met before. I did not know she had married a second time.

LADY MARKBY
[Genially.] Ah, nowadays people marry as often as they can, don't they? It is most fashionable. *[To DUCHESS OF MARYBOROUGH.]* Dear Duchess, and how is the Duke? Brain still weak, I suppose? Well, that is only to be expected, is it not? His good father was just the same. There is nothing like race, is there?

MRS. CHEVELEY
[Playing with her fan.] But have we really met before, Lady Chiltern? I can't remember where. I have been out of England for so long.

LADY CHILTERN We were at school together, Mrs. Cheveley.

MRS. CHEVELEY
[Superciliously.] Indeed? I have forgotten all about my schooldays. I have a vague impression that they were detestable.

LADY CHILTERN
[Coldly.] I am not surprised!

MRS. CHEVELEY
[In her sweetest manner.] Do you know, I am quite looking forward to meeting your clever husband, Lady Chiltern. Since he has been at the Foreign Office, he has been so much talked of in Vienna. They actually succeed

in spelling his name right in the newspapers. That in itself is fame, on the continent.

LADY CHILTERN
I hardly think there will be much in common between you and my husband, Mrs. Cheveley! *[Moves away.]*

VICOMTE DE NANJAC
Ah! chere Madame, queue surprise! I have not seen you since Berlin!

MRS. CHEVELEY
Not since Berlin, Vicomte. Five years ago!

VICOMTE DE NANJAC
And you are younger and more beautiful than ever. How do you manage it?

MRS. CHEVELEY
By making it a rule only to talk to perfectly charming people like yourself.

VICOMTE DE NANJAC
Ah! you flatter me. You butter me, as they say here.

MRS. CHEVELEY
Do they say that here? How dreadful of them!

VICOMTE DE NANJAC
Yes, they have a wonderful language. It should be more widely known.

[SIR ROBERT CHILTERN enters. A man of forty, but looking somewhat younger. Clean-shaven, with finely cut features, dark-haired and dark-eyed. A personality of mark. Not popular—few personalities are. But intensely admired by the few, and deeply respected by the many. The note of his manner is that of perfect distinction, with a slight touch of pride. One feels that he is conscious of the success he has made in life. A nervous temperament, with a tired look. The firmly chiseled mouth and chin contrast strikingly with the romantic expression in the deep set eyes. The variance is suggestive of an almost complete separation of passion and intellect, as though thought and emotion were each isolated in its own sphere through some violence of will-power. There is nervousness in the nostrils, and in the pale, thin, pointed hands. It would be inaccurate to call him picturesque. Picturesqueness cannot survive the House of Commons. But Vandyck would have liked to have painted his head.]

SIR ROBERT CHILTERN
Good evening, Lady Markby! I hope you have brought Sir John with you?

LADY MARKBY
Oh! I have brought a much more charming person than Sir John. Sir John's temper since he has taken seriously to politics has become quite unbearable. Really, now that the House of Commons is trying to become useful, it does a great deal of harm.

SIR ROBERT CHILTERN
I hope not, Lady Markby. At any rate we do our best to waste the public time, don't we? But who is this charming person you have been kind enough to bring to us?

LADY MARKBY
Her name is Mrs. Cheveley! One of the Dorsetshire Cheveleys, I suppose. But I really don't know. Families are so mixed nowadays. Indeed, as a rule, everybody turns out to be somebody else.

SIR ROBERT CHILTERN
Mrs. Cheveley? I seem to know the name.

LADY MARKBY
She has just arrived from Vienna.

SIR ROBERT CHILTERN
Ah! yes. I think I know whom you mean.

LADY MARKBY
Oh! she goes everywhere there, and has such pleasant scandals about all her friends. I really must go to Vienna next winter. I hope there is a good chef at the Embassy.

SIR ROBERT CHILTERN
If there is not, the Ambassador will certainly have to be recalled. Pray point out Mrs. Cheveley to me. I should like to see her.

LADY MARKBY
Let me introduce you. *[To MRS. CHEVELEY.]* My dear, Sir Robert Chiltern is dying to know you!

SIR ROBERT CHILTERN
[Bowing.] Everyone is dying to know the brilliant Mrs. Cheveley. Our attachés at Vienna write to us about nothing else.

MRS. CHEVELEY
Thank you, Sir Robert. An acquaintance that begins with a compliment is sure to develop into a real friendship. It starts in the right manner. And I find that I know Lady Chiltern already.

SIR ROBERT CHILTERN
Really?

MRS. CHEVELEY
Yes. She has just reminded me that we were at school together. I remember it perfectly now. She always got the good conduct prize. I have a distinct recollection of Lady Chiltern always getting the good conduct prize!

SIR ROBERT CHILTERN
[Smiling.] And what prizes did you get, Mrs. Cheveley?

MRS. CHEVELEY
My prizes came a little later on in life. I don't think any of them were for good conduct. I forget!

SIR ROBERT CHILTERN
I am sure they were for something charming!

MRS. CHEVELEY
I don't know that women are always rewarded for being charming. I think they are usually punished for it! Certainly, more women grow old nowadays through the faithfulness of their admirers than through anything else! At least that is the only way I can account for the terribly haggard look of most of your pretty women in London!

SIR ROBERT CHILTERN
What an appalling philosophy that sounds! To attempt to classify you, Mrs. Cheveley, would be an impertinence. But may I ask, at heart, are you an optimist or a pessimist? Those seem to be the only two fashionable religions left to us nowadays.

MRS. CHEVELEY
Oh, I'm neither. Optimism begins in a broad grin, and Pessimism ends with blue spectacles. Besides, they are both of them merely poses.

SIR ROBERT CHILTERN
You prefer to be natural?

MRS. CHEVELEY
Sometimes. But it is such a very difficult pose to keep up.

SIR ROBERT CHILTERN
What would those modern psychological novelists, of whom we hear so much, say to such a theory as that?

MRS. CHEVELEY
Ah! the strength of women comes from the fact that psychology cannot explain us. Men can be analyzed, women…merely adored.

SIR ROBERT CHILTERN
You think science cannot grapple with the problem of women?

MRS. CHEVELEY
Science can never grapple with the irrational. That is why it has no future before it, in this world.

SIR ROBERT CHILTERN
And women represent the irrational.

MRS. CHEVELEY
Well-dressed women do.

SIR ROBERT CHILTERN
[With a polite bow.] I fear I could hardly agree with you there. But do sit down. And now tell me, what makes you leave your brilliant Vienna for our gloomy London—or perhaps the question is indiscreet?

MRS. CHEVELEY
Questions are never indiscreet. Answers sometimes are.

SIR ROBERT CHILTERN
Well, at any rate, may I know if it is politics or pleasure?

MRS. CHEVELEY
Politics are my only pleasure. You see nowadays it is not fashionable to flirt till one is forty, or to be romantic till one is forty-five, so we poor women who are under thirty, or say we are, have nothing open to us but politics or philanthropy. And philanthropy seems to me to have become simply the refuge of people who wish to annoy their fellow creatures. I prefer politics. I think they are more…becoming!

SIR ROBERT CHILTERN
A political life is a noble career!

MRS. CHEVELEY
Sometimes. And sometimes it is a clever game, Sir Robert. And sometimes it is a great nuisance.

SIR ROBERT CHILTERN
Which do you find it?

MRS. CHEVELEY
I? A combination of all three. [Drops her fan.]

SIR ROBERT CHILTERN
[Picks up fan.] Allow me!

MRS. CHEVELEY
Thanks.

SIR ROBERT CHILTERN
But you have not told me yet what makes you honour London so suddenly. Our season is almost over.

MRS. CHEVELEY
Oh! I don't care about the London season! It is too matrimonial. People are either hunting for husbands, or hiding from them. I wanted to meet you. It is quite true. You know what a woman's curiosity is. Almost as great as a man's! I wanted immensely to meet you, and…to ask you to do something for me.

SIR ROBERT CHILTERN
I hope it is not a little thing, Mrs. Cheveley. I find that little things are so very difficult to do.

MRS. CHEVELEY
[After a moment's reflection.] No, I don't think it is quite a little thing.

SIR ROBERT CHILTERN
I am so glad. Do tell me what it is.

MRS. CHEVELEY
Later on. *[Rises.]* And now may I walk through your beautiful house? I hear your pictures are charming. Poor Baron Arnheim—you remember the Baron?—used to tell me you had some wonderful Corots.

SIR ROBERT CHILTERN
[With an almost imperceptible start.] Did you know Baron Arnheim well?

MRS. CHEVELEY
[Smiling.] Intimately. Did you?

SIR ROBERT CHILTERN
At one time.

MRS. CHEVELEY
Wonderful man, wasn't he?

SIR ROBERT CHILTERN
[After a pause.] He was very remarkable, in many ways.

MRS. CHEVELEY
I often think it such a pity he never wrote his memoirs. They would have been most interesting.

SIR ROBERT CHILTERN
Yes: he knew men and cities well, like the old Greek.

MRS. CHEVELEY
Without the dreadful disadvantage of having a Penelope waiting at home for him.

MASON
Lord Goring.

[Enter LORD GORING. Thirty-four, but always says he is younger. A well bred, expressionless face. He is clever, but would not like to be thought so. A flawless dandy, he would be annoyed if he were considered romantic. He plays with life, and is on perfectly good terms with the world. He is fond of being misunderstood. It gives him a post of vantage.]

SIR ROBERT CHILTERN
Good evening, my dear Arthur! Mrs. Cheveley, allow me to introduce to you Lord Goring, the idlest man in London.

MRS. CHEVELEY
I have met Lord Goring before.

LORD GORING
[Bowing.] I did not think you would remember me, Mrs. Cheveley.

MRS. CHEVELEY
My memory is under admirable control. And are you still a bachelor?

LORD GORING
I…believe so.

MRS. CHEVELEY
How very romantic!

LORD GORING
Oh! I am not at all romantic. I am not old enough. I leave romance to my seniors.

SIR ROBERT CHILTERN
Lord Goring is the result of Boodle's Club, Mrs. Cheveley.

MRS. CHEVELEY
He reflects every credit on the institution.

LORD GORING
May I ask are you staying in London long?

MRS. CHEVELEY
That depends partly on the weather, partly on the cooking, and partly on Sir Robert.

SIR ROBERT CHILTERN
You are not going to plunge us into a European war, I hope?

MRS. CHEVELEY
There is no danger, at present!

[She nods to LORD GORING, with a look of amusement in her eyes, and goes out with SIR ROBERT CHILTERN. LORD GORING saunters over to MABEL CHILTERN.]

MABEL CHILTERN
You are very late!

LORD GORING
Have you missed me?

MABEL CHILTERN
Awfully!

LORD GORING
Then I am sorry I did not stay away longer. I like being missed.

MABEL CHILTERN
How very selfish of you!

LORD GORING
I am very selfish.

MABEL CHILTERN
You are always telling me of your bad qualities, Lord Goring.

LORD GORING
I have only told you half of them as yet, Miss Mabel!

MABEL CHILTERN
Are the others very bad?

LORD GORING
Quite dreadful! When I think of them at night I go to sleep at once.

MABEL CHILTERN
Well, I delight in your bad qualities. I wouldn't have you part with one of them.

LORD GORING
How very nice of you! But then you are always nice. By the way, I want to ask you a question, Miss Mabel. Who brought Mrs. Cheveley here? That woman in heliotrope, who has just gone out of the room with your brother?

MABEL CHILTERN
Oh, I think Lady Markby brought her. Why do you ask?

LORD GORING
I haven't seen her for years, that is all.

MABEL CHILTERN
What an absurd reason!

LORD GORING
All reasons are absurd.

MABEL CHILTERN
What sort of a woman is she?

LORD GORING
Oh! a genius in the daytime and a beauty at night!

MABEL CHILTERN
I dislike her already.

LORD GORING
That shows your admirable good taste.

VICOMTE DE NANJAC
[Approaching.] Ah, the English young lady is the dragon of good taste, is she not? Quite the dragon of good taste.

LORD GORING
So the newspapers are always telling us.

VICOMTE DE NANJAC
I read all your English newspapers. I find them so amusing.

LORD GORING
Then, my dear Nanjac, you must certainly read between the lines.

VICOMTE DE NANJAC
I should like to, but my professor objects. *[To MABEL CHILTERN.]* May I have the pleasure of escorting you to the music-room, Mademoiselle?

MABEL CHILTERN
[Looking very disappointed.] Delighted, Vicomte, quite delighted! *[Turning to LORD GORING.]* Aren't you coming to the music-room?

LORD GORING
Not if there is any music going on, Miss Mabel.

MABEL CHILTERN
[Severely.] The music is in German. You would not understand it.

[Goes out with the VICOMTE DE NANJAC. LORD CAVERSHAM comes up to his son.]

LORD CAVERSHAM
Well, sir! what are you doing here? Wasting your life as usual! You should be in bed, sir. You keep too late hours! I heard of you the other night at Lady Rufford's dancing till four o'clock in the morning!

LORD GORING
Only a quarter to four, father.

LORD CAVERSHAM
Can't make out how you stand London Society. The thing has gone to the dogs, a lot of damned nobodies talking about nothing.

LORD GORING
I love talking about nothing, father. It is the only thing I know anything about.

LORD CAVERSHAM
You seem to me to be living entirely for pleasure.

LORD GORING
What else is there to live for, father? Nothing ages like happiness.

LORD CAVERSHAM
You are heartless, sir, very heartless!

LORD GORING
I hope not, father. Good evening, Lady Basildon!

LADY BASILDON
[Arching two pretty eyebrows.] Are you here? I had no idea you ever came to political parties!

LORD GORING
I adore political parties. They are the only place left to us where people don't talk politics.

LADY BASILDON
I delight in talking politics. I talk them all day long. But I can't bear listening to them. I don't know how the unfortunate men in the House stand these long debates.

LORD GORING
By never listening.

LADY BASILDON
Really?

LORD GORING
[In his most serious manner.] Of course. You see, it is a very dangerous thing to listen. If one listens one may be convinced; and a man who allows himself to be convinced by an argument is a thoroughly unreasonable person.

LADY BASILDON
Ah! that accounts for so much in men that I have never understood, and so much in women that their husbands never appreciate in them!

MRS. MARCHMONT
[With a sigh.] Our husbands never appreciate anything in us. We have to go to others for that!

LADY BASILDON
[Emphatically.] Yes, always to others, have we not?

LORD GORING
[Smiling.] And those are the views of the two ladies who are known to have the most admirable husbands in London.

MRS. MARCHMONT
That is exactly what we can't stand. My Reginald is quite hopelessly faultless. He is really unendurably so, at times! There is not the smallest element of excitement in knowing him.

LORD GORING
How terrible! Really, the thing should be more widely known!

LADY BASILDON
Basildon is quite as bad; he is as domestic as if he was a bachelor.

MRS. MARCHMONT
[Pressing LADY BASILDON'S hand.] My poor Olivia! We have married perfect husbands, and we are well punished for it.

LORD GORING
I should have thought it was the husbands who were punished.

MRS. MARCHMONT
[Drawing herself up.] Oh, dear no! They are as happy as possible! And as for trusting us, it is tragic how much they trust us.

LADY BASILDON
Perfectly tragic!

LORD GORING
Or comic, Lady Basildon?

LADY BASILDON
Certainly not comic, Lord Goring. How unkind of you to

suggest such a thing!

MRS. MARCHMONT
I am afraid Lord Goring is in the camp of the enemy, as usual. I saw him talking to that Mrs. Cheveley when he came in.

LORD GORING
Handsome woman, Mrs. Cheveley!

LADY BASILDON
[Stiffly.] Please don't praise other women in our presence. You might wait for us to do that!

LORD GORING
I did wait.

MRS. MARCHMONT
Well, we are not going to praise her. I hear she went to the Opera on Monday night, and told Tommy Rufford at supper that, as far as she could see, London Society was entirely made up of dowdies and dandies.

LORD GORING
She is quite right, too. The men are all dowdies and the women are all dandies, aren't they?

MRS. MARCHMONT
[After a pause.] Oh! do you really think that is what Mrs. Cheveley meant?

LORD GORING
Of course. And a very sensible remark for Mrs. Cheveley to make, too.

[Enter MABEL CHILTERN. She joins the group.]

MABEL CHILTERN
Why are you talking about Mrs. Cheveley? Everybody is talking about Mrs. Cheveley! Lord Goring says—what did you say, Lord Goring, about Mrs. Cheveley? Oh! I remember, that she was a genius in the daytime and a beauty at night.

LADY BASILDON
What a horrid combination! So very unnatural!

MRS. MARCHMONT
[In her most dreamy manner.] I like looking at geniuses, and listening to beautiful people.

LORD GORING
Ah! that is morbid of you, Mrs. Marchmont!

MRS. MARCHMONT
[Brightening to a look of real pleasure.] I am so glad to hear you say that. Marchmont and I have been married for seven years, and he has never once told me that I was morbid. Men are so painfully unobservant!

LADY BASILDON
[Turning to her.] I have always said, dear Margaret, that you were the most morbid person in London.

MRS. MARCHMONT
Ah! but you are always sympathetic, Olivia!

MABEL CHILTERN
Is it morbid to have a desire for food? I have a great desire for food. Lord Goring, will you give me some supper?

LORD GORING
With pleasure, Miss Mabel. *[Moves away with her.]*

MABEL CHILTERN
How horrid you have been! You have never talked to me the whole evening!

LORD GORING
How could I? You went away with the child-diplomatist.

MABEL CHILTERN
You might have followed us. Pursuit would have been only polite. I don't think I like you at all this evening!

LORD GORING
I like you immensely.

MABEL CHILTERN
Well, I wish you'd show it in a more marked way! *[They go downstairs.]*

MRS. MARCHMONT
Olivia, I have a curious feeling of absolute faintness. I think I should like some supper very much. I know I should like some supper.

LADY BASILDON
I am positively dying for supper, Margaret!

MRS. MARCHMONT
Men are so horribly selfish, they never think of these things.

LADY BASILDON
Men are grossly material, grossly material!

[The VICOMTE DE NANJAC enters from the music-room with some other guests. After having carefully examined all the people present, he approaches LADY BASILDON.]

VICOMTE DE NANJAC
May I have the honour of taking you down to supper, Comtesse?

LADY BASILDON
[Coldly.] I never take supper, thank you, Vicomte. *[The VICOMTE is about to retire. LADY BASILDON, seeing this, rises at once and takes his arm.]* But I will come down with you with pleasure.

VICOMTE DE NANJAC
I am so fond of eating! I am very English in all my tastes.

LADY BASILDON
You look quite English, Vicomte, quite English.

[They pass out. MR. MONTFORD, a perfectly groomed young dandy, approaches MRS. MARCHMONT.]

MR. MONTFORD
Like some supper, Mrs. Marchmont?

MRS. MARCHMONT
[Languidly.] Thank you, Mr. Montford, I never touch supper. [Rises hastily and takes his arm.] But I will sit beside you, and watch you.

MR. MONTFORD
I don't know that I like being watched when I am eating!

MRS. MARCHMONT
Then I will watch someone else.

MR. MONTFORD
I don't know that I should like that either.

MRS. MARCHMONT
[Severely.] Pray, Mr. Montford, do not make these painful scenes of jealousy in public!

[They go downstairs with the other guests, passing SIR ROBERT CHILTERN and MRS. CHEVELEY, who now enter.]

SIR ROBERT CHILTERN
And are you going to any of our country houses before you leave England, Mrs. Cheveley?

MRS. CHEVELEY
Oh, no! I can't stand your English house parties. In England people actually try to be brilliant at breakfast. That is so dreadful of them! Only dull people are brilliant at breakfast. And then the family skeleton is always reading family prayers. My stay in England really depends on you, Sir Robert. *[Sits down on the sofa.]*

SIR ROBERT CHILTERN
[Taking a seat beside her.] Seriously?

MRS. CHEVELEY
Quite seriously. I want to talk to you about a great political and financial scheme, about this Argentine Canal Company, in fact.

SIR ROBERT CHILTERN
What a tedious, practical subject for you to talk about, Mrs. Cheveley!

MRS. CHEVELEY
Oh, I like tedious, practical subjects. What I don't like are tedious, practical people. There is a wide difference. Besides, you are interested, I know, in International Canal schemes. You were Lord Radley's secretary, weren't you, when the Government bought the Suez Canal shares?

SIR ROBERT CHILTERN
Yes. But the Suez Canal was a very great and splendid undertaking. It gave us our direct route to India. It had imperial value. It was necessary that we should have control. This Argentine scheme is a commonplace Stock Exchange swindle.

MRS. CHEVELEY
A speculation, Sir Robert! A brilliant, daring speculation.

SIR ROBERT CHILTERN
Believe me, Mrs. Cheveley, it is a swindle. Let us call things by their proper names. It makes matters simpler. We have all the information about it at the Foreign Office. In fact, I sent out a special Commission to inquire into the matter privately, and they report that the works are hardly begun, and as for the money already subscribed, no one seems to know what has become of it. The whole thing is a second Panama, and with not a quarter of the chance of success that miserable affair ever had. I hope you have not invested in it. I am sure you are far too clever to have done that.

MRS. CHEVELEY
I have invested very largely in it.

SIR ROBERT CHILTERN
Who could have advised you to do such a foolish thing?

MRS. CHEVELEY
Your old friend—and mine.

SIR ROBERT CHILTERN
Who?

MRS. CHEVELEY
Baron Arnheim.

SIR ROBERT CHILTERN
[Frowning.] Ah! yes. I remember hearing, at the time of his death, that he had been mixed up in the whole affair.

MRS. CHEVELEY
It was his last romance. His last but one, to do him justice.

SIR ROBERT CHILTERN
[Rising.] But you have not seen my Corots yet. They are in the music room. Corots seem to go with music, don't they? May I show them to you?

MRS. CHEVELEY
[Shaking her head.] I am not in a mood tonight for silver twilights, or rose-pink dawns. I want to talk business. *[Motions to him with her fan to sit down again beside her.]*

SIR ROBERT CHILTERN
I fear I have no advice to give you, Mrs. Cheveley, except to interest yourself in something less dangerous. The success of the Canal depends, of course, on the attitude of England, and I am going to lay the report of the Commissioners before the House tomorrow night.

MRS. CHEVELEY
That you must not do. In your own interests, Sir Robert, to say nothing of mine, you must not do that.

SIR ROBERT CHILTERN
[Looking at her in wonder.] In my own interests? My dear Mrs. Cheveley, what do you mean? *[Sits down beside her.]*

MRS. CHEVELEY
Sir Robert, I will be quite frank with you. I want you to withdraw the report that you had intended to lay before the House, on the ground that you have reasons to believe that the Commissioners have been prejudiced or misinformed, or something. Then I want you to say a few words to the effect that the Government is going to reconsider the question, and that you have reason to believe that the Canal, if completed, will be of great international value. You know the sort of things ministers say in cases of this kind. A few ordinary platitudes will do. In modern life nothing produces such an effect as a good platitude. It makes the whole world kin. Will you do that for me?

SIR ROBERT CHILTERN
Mrs. Cheveley, you cannot be serious in making me such a proposition!

MRS. CHEVELE
I am quite serious.

SIR ROBERT CHILTERN
[Coldly.] Pray allow me to believe that you are not.

MRS. CHEVELEY
[Speaking with great deliberation and emphasis.] Ah! but I am. And if you do what I ask you, I...will pay you very handsomely!

SIR ROBERT CHILTERN
Pay me!

MRS. CHEVELEY
Yes.

SIR ROBERT CHILTERN
I am afraid I don't quite understand what you mean.

MRS. CHEVELEY
[Leaning back on the sofa and looking at him.] How very disappointing! And I have come all the way from Vienna in order that you should thoroughly understand me.

SIR ROBERT CHILTERN
I fear I don't.

MRS. CHEVELEY
[In her most nonchalant manner.] My dear Sir Robert, you are a man of the world, and you have your price, I suppose. Everybody has nowadays. The drawback is that most people are so dreadfully expensive. I know I am. I hope you will be more reasonable in your terms.

SIR ROBERT CHILTERN
[Rises indignantly.] If you will allow me, I will call your carriage for you. You have lived so long abroad, Mrs. Cheveley, that you seem to be unable to realise that you are talking to an English gentleman.

MRS. CHEVELEY
[Detains him by touching his arm with her fan, and keeping it there while she is talking.] I realise that I am talking to a man who laid the foundation of his fortune by selling to a Stock Exchange speculator a Cabinet secret.

SIR ROBERT CHILTERN
[Biting his lip.] What do you mean?

MRS. CHEVELEY
[Rising and facing him.] I mean that I know the real origin of your wealth and your career, and I have got your letter, too.

SIR ROBERT CHILTERN
What letter?

MRS. CHEVELEY
[Contemptuously.] The letter you wrote to Baron Arnheim, when you were Lord Radley's secretary, telling the Baron to buy Suez Canal shares—a letter written three days before the Government announced its own purchase.

SIR ROBERT CHILTERN
[Hoarsely.] It is not true.

MRS. CHEVELEY
You thought that letter had been destroyed. How foolish of you! It is in my possession.

SIR ROBERT CHILTERN
The affair to which you allude was no more than a speculation. The House of Commons had not yet passed the bill; it might have been rejected.

MRS. CHEVELEY
It was a swindle, Sir Robert. Let us call things by their proper names. It makes everything simpler. And now I am going to sell you that letter, and the price I ask for it is your public support of the Argentine scheme. You made your own fortune out of one canal. You must help me and my friends to make our fortunes out of another!

SIR ROBERT CHILTERN
It is infamous, what you propose—infamous!

MRS. CHEVELEY
Oh, no! This is the game of life as we all have to play it, Sir Robert, sooner or later!

SIR ROBERT CHILTERN
I cannot do what you ask me.

MRS. CHEVELEY
You mean you cannot help doing it. You know you are standing on the edge of a precipice. And it is not for you to make terms. It is for you to accept them. Supposing you refuse—

SIR ROBERT CHILTERN
What then?

MRS. CHEVELEY
My dear Sir Robert, what then? You are ruined, that is all! Remember to what a point your Puritanism in England has brought you. In old days nobody pretended to be a bit better than his neighbours. In fact, to be a bit better than one's neighbour was considered excessively vulgar and middle class. Nowadays, with our modern mania for morality, everyone has to pose as a paragon of purity, incorruptibility, and all the other seven deadly virtues— and what is the result? You all go over like ninepins—one after the other. Not a year passes in England without somebody disappearing. Scandals used to lend charm, or at least interest, to a man—now they crush him. And yours is a very nasty scandal. You couldn't survive it. If it were known that as a young man, secretary to a great and important minister, you sold a Cabinet secret for a large sum of money, and that that was the origin of your wealth and career, you would be hounded out of public life, you would disappear completely. And after all, Sir Robert, why should you sacrifice your entire future rather than deal diplomatically with your enemy? For the moment I am your enemy. I admit it! And I am much stronger than you are. The big battalions are on my side. You have a splendid position, but it is your splendid position that makes you so vulnerable. You can't defend it! And I am in attack. Of course I have not talked morality to you. You must admit in fairness that I have spared you that. Years ago you did a clever, unscrupulous thing; it turned out a great success. You owe to it your fortune and position. And now you have got to pay for it. Sooner or later we have all to pay for what we do. You have to pay now. Before I leave you tonight, you have got to promise me to suppress your report, and to speak in the House in favour of this scheme.

SIR ROBERT CHILTERN
What you ask is impossible.

MRS. CHEVELEY
You must make it possible. You are going to make it possible. Sir Robert, you know what your English newspapers are like. Suppose that when I leave this house I drive down to some newspaper office, and give them this scandal and the proofs of it! Think of their loathsome joy, of the delight they would have in dragging you down, of the mud and mire they would plunge you in. Think of the hypocrite with his greasy smile penning his leading article, and arranging the foulness of the public placard.

SIR ROBERT CHILTERN
Stop! You want me to withdraw the report and to make a short speech stating that I believe there are possibilities in the scheme?

MRS. CHEVELEY
[Sitting down on the sofa.] Those are my terms.

SIR ROBERT CHILTERN
[In a low voice.] I will give you any sum of money you want.

MRS. CHEVELEY
Even you are not rich enough, Sir Robert, to buy back your past. No man is.

SIR ROBERT CHILTERN
I will not do what you ask me. I will not.

MRS. CHEVELEY
You have to. If you don't...[Rises from the sofa.]

SIR ROBERT CHILTERN
[Bewildered and unnerved.] Wait a moment! What did you propose? You said that you would give me back my letter, didn't you?

MRS. CHEVELEY
Yes. That is agreed. I will be in the Ladies' Gallery to-morrow night at half-past eleven. If by that time—and you will have had heaps of opportunity—you have made an announcement to the House in the terms I wish, I shall hand you back your letter with the prettiest thanks, and the best, or at any rate the most suitable, compliment I can think of. I intend to play quite fairly with you. One should always play fairly...when one has the winning cards. The Baron taught me that...amongst other things.

SIR ROBERT CHILTERN
You must let me have time to consider your proposal.

MRS. CHEVELEY
No; you must settle now!

SIR ROBERT CHILTERN
Give me a week—three days!

MRS. CHEVELEY
Impossible! I have got to telegraph to Vienna tonight.

SIR ROBERT CHILTERN
My God! what brought you into my life?

MRS. CHEVELEY
Circumstances. [Moves towards the door.]

SIR ROBERT CHILTERN
Don't go. I consent. The report shall be withdrawn. I will arrange for a question to be put to me on the subject.

MRS. CHEVELEY
Thank you. I knew we should come to an amicable agreement. I understood your nature from the first. I analysed you, though you did not adore me. And now you can get my carriage for me, Sir Robert. I see the people coming up from supper, and Englishmen always get romantic after a meal, and that bores me dreadfully. [Exit SIR ROBERT CHILTERN.]

[Enter Guests, LADY CHILTERN, LADY MARKBY, LORD CAVERSHAM, LADY BASILDON, MRS. MARCHMONT, VICOMTE DE NANJAC, MR. MONTFORD.]

LADY MARKBY
Well, dear Mrs. Cheveley, I hope you have enjoyed yourself. Sir Robert is very entertaining, is he not?

MRS. CHEVELEY
Most entertaining! I have enjoyed my talk with him immensely.

LADY MARKBY
He has had a very interesting and brilliant career. And he has married a most admirable wife. Lady Chiltern is a woman of the very highest principles, I am glad to say. I am a little too old now, myself, to trouble about setting a good example, but I always admire people who do. And Lady Chiltern has a very ennobling effect on life, though her dinner parties are rather dull sometimes. But one can't have everything, can one? And now I must go, dear. Shall I call for you tomorrow?

MRS. CHEVELEY
Thanks.

LADY MARKBY
We might drive in the Park at five. Everything looks so fresh in the Park now!

MRS. CHEVELEY
Except the people!

LADY MARKBY
Perhaps the people are a little jaded. I have often observed that the Season as it goes on produces a kind of softening of the brain. However, I think anything is better than high intellectual pressure. That is the most unbecoming thing there is. It makes the noses of the young girls so particularly large. And there is nothing so difficult to marry as a large nose; men don't like them. Goodnight, dear! [To LADY CHILTERN.] Goodnight, Gertrude! [Goes out on LORD CAVERSHAM'S arm.]

MRS. CHEVELEY
What a charming house you have, Lady Chiltern! I have spent a delightful evening. It has been so interesting getting to know your husband.

LADY CHILTERN
Why did you wish to meet my husband, Mrs. Cheveley?

MRS. CHEVELEY
Oh, I will tell you. I wanted to interest him in this Argentine Canal scheme, of which I dare say you have heard. And I found him most susceptible—susceptible to reason, I mean. A rare thing in a man. I converted him in ten minutes. He is going to make a speech in the House tomorrow night in favour of the idea. We must go to the Ladies' Gallery and hear him! It will be a great occasion!

LADY CHILTERN
There must be some mistake. That scheme could never have my husband's support.

MRS. CHEVELEY
Oh, I assure you it's all settled. I don't regret my tedious journey from Vienna now. It has been a great success. But, of course, for the next twenty-four hours the whole thing is a dead secret.

LADY CHILTERN
[Gently.] A secret? Between whom?

MRS. CHEVELEY
[With a flash of amusement in her eyes.] Between your husband and myself.

SIR ROBERT CHILTERN
[Entering.] Your carriage is here, Mm Cheveley!

MRS. CHEVELEY
Thanks! Good evening, Lady Chiltern! Goodnight, Lord Goring! I am at Claridge's. Don't you think you might leave a card?

LORD GORING
If you wish it, Mrs. Cheveley!

MRS. CHEVELEY
Oh, don't be so solemn about it, or I shall be obliged to leave a card on you. In England I suppose that would hardly be considered EN REGLE. Abroad, we are more civilised. Will you see me down, Sir Robert? Now that we have both the same interests at heart we shall be great friends, I hope!

[Sails out on SIR ROBERT CHILTERN'S arm. LADY CHILTERN goes to the top of the staircase and looks down at them as they descend. Her expression is troubled. After a little time she is joined by some of the guests, and passes with them into another reception room.]

MABEL CHILTERN
What a horrid woman!

LORD GORING
You should go to bed, Miss Mabel.

MABEL CHILTERN
Lord Goring!

LORD GORING
My father told me to go to bed an hour ago. I don't see why I shouldn't give you the same advice. I always pass on good advice. It is the only thing to do with it. It is never of any use to oneself.

MABEL CHILTERN
Lord Goring, you are always ordering me out of the room. I think it most courageous of you. Especially as I am not going to bed for hours. *[Goes over to the sofa.]* You can come and sit down if you like, and talk about anything in the world, except the Royal Academy, Mrs. Cheveley, or novels in Scotch dialect. They are not improving subjects. *[Catches sight of something that is lying on the sofa half hidden by the cushion.]* What is this? Some one has dropped a diamond brooch! Quite beautiful, isn't it? *[Shows it to him.]* I wish it was mine, but Gertrude won't let me wear anything but pearls, and I am thoroughly sick of pearls. They make one look so plain, so good and so intellectual. I wonder whom the brooch belongs to.

LORD GORING
I wonder who dropped it.

MABEL CHILTERN
It is a beautiful brooch.

LORD GORING
It is a handsome bracelet.

MABEL CHILTERN
It isn't a bracelet. It's a brooch.

LORD GORING
It can be used as a bracelet. *[Takes it from her, and, pulling out a green letter-case, puts the ornament carefully in it, and replaces the whole thing in his breast-pocket with the most perfect sang froid.]*

MABEL CHILTERN
What are you doing?

LORD GORING
Miss Mabel, I am going to make a rather strange request to you.

MABEL CHILTERN
[Eagerly.] Oh, pray do! I have been waiting for it all the evening.

LORD GORING
[Is a little taken aback, but recovers himself.] Don't mention to anybody that I have taken charge of this brooch. Should any one write and claim it, let me know at once.

MABEL CHILTERN
That is a strange request.

LORD GORING
Well, you see I gave this brooch to somebody once, years ago.

MABEL CHILTERN
You did?

LORD GORING
Yes.

[LADY CHILTERN enters alone. The other guests have gone.]

MABEL CHILTERN
Then I shall certainly bid you goodnight. Goodnight, Gertrude! *[Exit.]*

LADY CHILTERN
Goodnight, dear! *[To LORD GORING.]* You saw whom Lady Markby brought here tonight?

LORD GORING
Yes. It was an unpleasant surprise. What did she come here for?

LADY CHILTERN
Apparently to try and lure Robert to uphold some fraudulent scheme in which she is interested. The Argentine Canal, in fact.

LORD GORING
She has mistaken her man, hasn't she?

LADY CHILTERN
She is incapable of understanding an upright nature like my husband's!

LORD GORING
Yes. I should fancy she came to grief if she tried to get Robert into her toils. It is extraordinary what astounding mistakes clever women make.

LADY CHILTERN
I don't call women of that kind clever. I call them stupid!

LORD GORING
Same thing often. Goodnight, Lady Chiltern!

LADY CHILTERN
Goodnight!

[Enter SIR ROBERT CHILTERN.]

SIR ROBERT CHILTERN
My dear Arthur, you are not going? Do stop a little!

LORD GORING
Afraid I can't, thanks. I have promised to look in at the Hartlocks'. I believe they have got a mauve Hungarian band that plays mauve Hungarian music. See you soon. Goodbye!

[Exit.]

SIR ROBERT CHILTERN
How beautiful you look tonight, Gertrude!

LADY CHILTERN
Robert, it is not true, is it? You are not going to lend your support to this Argentine speculation? You couldn't!

SIR ROBERT CHILTERN
[Starting.] Who told you I intended to do so?

LADY CHILTERN
That woman who has just gone out, Mrs. Cheveley, as she calls herself now. She seemed to taunt me with it. Robert, I know this woman. You don't. We were at school together. She was untruthful, dishonest, an evil influence on every one whose trust or friendship she could win. I hated, I despised her. She stole things, she was a thief. She was sent away for being a thief. Why do you let her influence you?

SIR ROBERT CHILTERN
Gertrude, what you tell me may be true, but it happened many years ago. It is best forgotten! Mrs. Cheveley may

have changed since then. No one should be entirely judged by their past.

LADY CHILTERN
[Sadly.] One's past is what one is. It is the only way by which people should be judged.

SIR ROBERT CHILTERN
That is a hard saying, Gertrude!

LADY CHILTERN
It is a true saying, Robert. And what did she mean by boasting that she had got you to lend your support, your name, to a thing I have heard you describe as the most dishonest and fraudulent scheme there has ever been in political life?

SIR ROBERT CHILTERN
[Biting his lip.] I was mistaken in the view I took. We all may make mistakes.

LADY CHILTERN
But you told me yesterday that you had received the report from the Commission, and that it entirely condemned the whole thing.

SIR ROBERT CHILTERN
[Walking up and down.] I have reasons now to believe that the Commission was prejudiced, or, at any rate, misinformed. Besides, Gertrude, public and private life are different things. They have different laws, and move on different lines.

LADY CHILTERN
They should both represent man at his highest. I see no difference between them.

SIR ROBERT CHILTERN
[Stopping.] In the present case, on a matter of practical politics, I have changed my mind. That is all.

LADY CHILTERN
All!

SIR ROBERT CHILTERN
[Sternly.] Yes!

LADY CHILTERN
Robert! Oh! it is horrible that I should have to ask you such a question—Robert, are you telling me the whole truth?

SIR ROBERT CHILTERN
Why do you ask me such a question?

LADY CHILTERN
[After a pause.] Why do you not answer it?

SIR ROBERT CHILTERN
[Sitting down.] Gertrude, truth is a very complex thing, and politics is a very complex business. There are wheels within wheels. One may be under certain obligations to people that one must pay. Sooner or later in political life one has to compromise. Everyone does.

LADY CHILTERN
Compromise? Robert, why do you talk so differently tonight from the way I have always heard you talk? Why are you changed?

SIR ROBERT CHILTERN
I am not changed. But circumstances alter things.

LADY CHILTERN
Circumstances should never alter principles!

SIR ROBERT CHILTERN
But if I told you—

LADY CHILTERN
What?

SIR ROBERT CHILTERN
That it was necessary, vitally necessary?

LADY CHILTERN
It can never be necessary to do what is not honourable. Or if it be necessary, then what is it that I have loved! But it is not, Robert; tell me it is not. Why should it be? What gain would you get? Money? We have no need of that! And money that comes from a tainted source is a degradation. Power? But power is nothing in itself. It is power to do good that is fine—that, and that only. What is it, then? Robert, tell me why you are going to do this dishonourable thing!

SIR ROBERT CHILTERN
Gertrude, you have no right to use that word. I told you it was a question of rational compromise. It is no more than that.

LADY CHILTERN
Robert, that is all very well for other men, for men who treat life simply as a sordid speculation; but not for you, Robert, not for you. You are different. All your life you have stood apart from others. You have never let the world soil you. To the world, as to myself, you have been an ideal always. Oh! be that ideal still. That great inheritance throw not away—that tower of ivory do not destroy. Robert,

men can love what is beneath them—things unworthy, stained, dishonoured. We women worship when we love; and when we lose our worship, we lose everything. Oh! don't kill my love for you, don't kill that!

SIR ROBERT CHILTERN
Gertrude!

LADY CHILTERN
I know that there are men with horrible secrets in their lives—men who have done some shameful thing, and who in some critical moment have to pay for it, by doing some other act of shame—oh! don't tell me you are such as they are! Robert, is there in your life any secret dishonour or disgrace? Tell me, tell me at once, that—

SIR ROBERT CHILTERN
That what?

LADY CHILTERN
[Speaking very slowly.] That our lives may drift apart.

SIR ROBERT CHILTERN
Drift apart?

LADY CHILTERN
That they may be entirely separate. It would be better for us both.

SIR ROBERT CHILTERN
Gertrude, there is nothing in my past life that you might not know.

LADY CHILTERN
I was sure of it, Robert, I was sure of it. But why did you say those dreadful things, things so unlike your real self? Don't let us ever talk about the subject again. You will write, won't you, to Mrs. Cheveley, and tell her that you cannot support this scandalous scheme of hers? If you have given her any promise you must take it back, that is all!

SIR ROBERT CHILTERN
Must I write and tell her that?

LADY CHILTERN
Surely, Robert! What else is there to do?

SIR ROBERT CHILTERN
I might see her personally. It would be better.

LADY CHILTERN
You must never see her again, Robert. She is not a woman you should ever speak to. She is not worthy to talk to a man like you. No; you must write to her at once, now, this moment, and let your letter show her that your decision is quite irrevocable!

SIR ROBERT CHILTERN
Write this moment!

LADY CHILTERN
Yes.

SIR ROBERT CHILTERN
But it is so late. It is close on twelve.

LADY CHILTERN
That makes no matter. She must know at once that she has been mistaken in you—and that you are not a man to do anything base or underhand or dishonourable. Write here, Robert. Write that you decline to support this scheme of hers, as you hold it to be a dishonest scheme. Yes—write the word dishonest. She knows what that word means. *[SIR ROBERT CHILTERN sits down and writes a letter. His wife takes it up and reads it.]* Yes; that will do. *[Rings bell.]* And now the envelope. *[He writes the envelope slowly. Enter MASON.]* Have this letter sent at once to Claridge's Hotel. There is no answer. *[Exit MASON. LADY CHILTERN kneels down beside her husband, and puts her arms around him.]* Robert, love gives one an instinct to things. I feel tonight that I have saved you from something that might have been a danger to you, from something that might have made men honour you less than they do. I don't think you realise sufficiently, Robert, that you have brought into the political life of our time a nobler atmosphere, a finer attitude towards life, a freer air of purer aims and higher ideals—I know it, and for that I love you, Robert.

SIR ROBERT CHILTERN
Oh, love me always, Gertrude, love me always!

LADY CHILTERN
I will love you always, because you will always be worthy of love. We needs must love the highest when we see it! *[Kisses him and rises and goes out.]*

[SIR ROBERT CHILTERN walks up and down for a moment; then sits down and buries his face in his hands. The Servant enters and begins pulling out the lights. SIR ROBERT CHILTERN looks up.]

SIR ROBERT CHILTERN
Put out the lights, Mason, put out the lights!

[The Servant puts out the lights. The room becomes almost dark. The only light there is comes from the great chandelier that hangs over the staircase and illumines the tapestry of the Triumph of Love.]

LESSON TWELVE

Objectives:

1. To review some of the key ideas of the Victorian Era, the Aesthetic Movement, and Oscar Wilde's life
2. To determine to what extent Wilde's life and the socio-political context of the play influenced *The Importance of Being Earnest*

Activity 1:

Copy and distribute Writing Assignment #2 (Persuade), which discusses the influence of the Victorian Era, The Aesthetic Movement, and Oscar Wilde's life on *The Importance of Being Earnest*. Return to the list of themes and motifs that the class created before reading the play, and hold a brief class discussion about which ones actually surfaced. While your students may incorporate some of the ideas the class discusses in their essays, encourage them to also present their own, unique arguments in their writing.

Activity 2:

If there is time at the end of class, have students continue to work on the group project. In addition, schedule which day each group will perform, and encourage the students to plan to meet sometime outside of class to complete the script, acquire the props and costume articles they need, and rehearse before the performance day.

It is recommended that you schedule the group performances so that they are in sequential order. Scenes in Acts I and II could be presented on the first day of performances, and scenes in Act III could be presented on the second.

WRITING ASSIGNMENT #2 - *The Importance of Being Earnest*

Persuade: Authorial Motivation in *The Importance of Being Earnest*

Prompt:

Even though some literary critics believe that works of art are completely isolated and have unique identities, others argue that art cannot be properly understood and evaluated without considering the author or the time period in which it was written or created.

In a well-organized essay, determine how much influence Oscar Wilde's life, the Victorian Era, and the Aesthetic Movement had on the play. Make sure that your argument is supported by examples from the text.

Pre-Writing:

Review what you know about the late 19th century, and write down some important ideas about the Aesthetic Movement, Victorian Era, and Oscar Wilde's life. Then, scan through the text, and record examples that show how each idea may have influenced the play.

If your argument is that the time period and Wilde's life had no influence on the play, find examples that show either that the play supported contrasting viewpoints to those of Wilde and of the Victorian Era, or show what could have been included in the play if those ideas did have influence.

Drafting:

Introduce your topic in the first paragraph, being sure to end it with a thesis statement. Then, write several body paragraphs, each addressing a key concept of the Victorian Era, the Aesthetic Movement, or Wilde's life and showing how it is incorporated in the play. Conclude your essay by showing how each of component of your argument ties into your thesis statement.

Peer Conference/Revising:

When you finish the rough draft of your composition, ask a student who sits near you to read it. After reading your draft, your classmate should tell you what he or she liked best about your work, which parts were difficult to understand, and ways in which your work could be improved. Reread your paper considering your classmate's comments, and make the corrections you think are necessary.

Proofreading/Editing:

Do a final proofreading of your essay, double-checking your grammar, spelling, organization, and the clarity of your ideas.

LESSON THIRTEEN

Objectives:

1. To practice writing essays in which students express their personal opinions
2. To relate a motif in the novel to personal experience

Activity 1:

Copy and distribute Writing Assignment #3 (Personal Opinion). Have students complete the assignment individually. If students need help brainstorming ideas for their essays, you could have a class discussion about the factors that go into creating personal identity.

Activity 2:

At this point, performance groups should have their scripts completely written and should be working on rehearsing their plays. If there is time at the end of class, you could allow the class to break into groups and rehearse their scenes.

WRITING ASSIGNMENT #3 - *The Importance of Being Earnest*

Personal Opinion: The Shaping of Personal Identity

Prompt:

The Importance of Being Earnest focuses greatly on issues of personal identity. Jack, not wanting his ward to view the carefree, hedonistic aspect of his personality, creates the alter ego of Ernest, who he uses as an excuse to leave the country and whose identity he assumes when he is in the city. Cecily develops Ernest's identity by making assumptions about his character and recording her imaginary interaction with him in her diary. Algernon makes Ernest's character even more complex by pretending to be him when he comes to Jack's country estate. In essence, Ernest is given an identity even though he does not exist as a physical person, suggesting that identity is a complicated issue and not synonymous with existence.

How are personal identities formed? How much choice does an individual have in how he or she is viewed, and how much influence do the opinions of other people have in shaping how a person understands him or herself? How does the environment in which a person lives affect his or her character?

In a well-organized essay, explain how you believe personal identity is created and developed.

Pre-Writing:

Think about what sort of factors influenced how you view yourself. Write these down. Then, determine how many of these factors are universal. You may use the play for additional examples, but do not feel as though your argument needs to agree with or rely on the text.

Drafting:

Introduce your topic in the first paragraph, being sure to end it with a thesis statement. Then, write several body paragraphs, each addressing key factors Conclude your essay by showing how each component of your argument ties into your thesis statement.

Peer Conference/Revising:

When you finish the rough draft of your composition, ask a student who sits near you to read it. After reading your draft, your classmate should tell you what he or she liked best about your work, which parts were difficult to understand, and ways in which your work could be improved. Reread your paper considering your classmate's comments, and make the corrections you think are necessary.

Proofreading/Editing:

Do a final proofreading of your essay, double-checking your grammar, spelling, organization, and the clarity of your ideas.

LESSON FOURTEEN

Objectives:

1. To have students perform their modern-day interpretations of *The Importance of Being Earnest* in front of the class

Activity 1:

Have the groups perform their scenes in front of the class. You could grade the students by completing the Group Presentation Evaluation Sheet that follows Lesson Seven. Ideally, the groups for Acts I and II should perform today.

LESSON FIFTEEN

Objectives:

1. To have students perform their modern-day interpretations of *the Importance of Being Earnest* in front of the class
2. To review all of the vocabulary in this unit

Activity 1:

Have the remaining groups perform their scenes in front of the class. You could grade the students by completing the Group Presentation Evaluation Sheet that follows Lesson Seven. Ideally, the group for Act III should perform today.

Activity 2:

Choose one (or more) of the vocabulary review activities listed below, and spend your class period as directed in the activity. Some of the materials for these review activities are located in the Vocabulary Resource Materials section in this LitPlan.

Vocabulary Review Activities:

1. Divide your class into two teams and have an old-fashioned spelling or definition bee.

2. Give each of your students (or students in groups of two, three or four) a *The Importance of Being Earnest* Vocabulary Word Search Puzzle. The person (group) to find all of the vocabulary words in the puzzle first wins.

3. Give students a *The Importance of Being Earnest* Vocabulary Word Search Puzzle without the word list. The person or group to find the most vocabulary words in the puzzle wins.

4. Use a *The Importance of Being Earnest* Vocabulary Crossword Puzzle. Put the puzzle onto a transparency on the overhead projector (so everyone can see it), and do the puzzle together as a class.

5. Give students a *The Importance of Being Earnest* Vocabulary Matching Worksheet to do.

6. Divide your class into two teams. Use *The Importance of Being Earnest* vocabulary words with their letters jumbled as a word list. Student 1 from Team A faces off against Student 1 from Team B. You write the first jumbled word on the board. The first student (1A or 1B) to unscramble the word wins the chance for his or her team to score points. If 1A wins the jumble, go to student 2A, and give him or her a definition. The student must give you the correct spelling of the vocabulary word that fits the definition. If he or she does, Team A scores a point, and you give student 3A a definition for which you expect a correctly spelled matching vocabulary word. Continue giving Team A definitions until some team member makes an incorrect response. An incorrect response sends the game back to the jumbled-word face off, this time with students 2A and 2B. Instead of repeating giving definitions to the first few students of each team, continue with the student after the one who gave the last incorrect response on the team. For example, if Team B wins the jumbled-word face-off, and student 5B gave the last incorrect answer for Team B, you would start this round of definition questions with student 6B, and so on. The team with the most points wins!

7. Have students write a story in which they correctly use as many vocabulary words as possible. Have students read their compositions orally. Post the most original compositions on your bulletin board.

LESSON SIXTEEN

Objectives:

1. To review the main ideas and events in *The Importance of Being Earnest*

Activity 1:

Choose one of the review games/activities suggested in this unit, and spend your class time as directed there.

Review Games/Activities:

1. Ask the class to make up a unit test for *The Importance of Being Earnest*. The test should have four sections: matching, true/false, short answer, and essay. Students may use half of the period to make the test and then swap papers and use the other half of the class period to take a test a classmate has devised (open book). You may want to use the unit test included in this packet or take questions from the students' unit tests to formulate your own test.

2. Take half of the period for students to make up true and false questions (including the answers). Collect the papers, and divide the class into two teams. Draw a big tic-tac-toe board on the chalkboard. Make one team X and one team O. Ask questions to each side, giving each student one turn. If the question is answered correctly, that student's team's letter (X or O) is placed in the box. If the answer is incorrect, no letter is placed in the box. The object is to get three in a row, like tic-tac-toe. You may want to keep track of the number of games won for each team.

3. Take half of the period for students to make up questions (true/false and short answer). Collect the questions. Divide the class into two teams. You'll alternate asking questions to individual members of teams A & B (like in a spelling bee). The question keeps going from A to B until it is correctly answered; then, a new question is asked. A correct answer does not allow the team to get another question. Correct answers are +2 points; incorrect answers are -1 point.

4. Have students pair up and quiz each other from their study guides and class notes.

5. Give students a *The Importance of Being Earnest* Crossword Puzzle to complete.

6. Play What's My Line? This is similar to the old television show. Students assume the roles of different characters from the story. One student gives clues to the class or to a panel of contestants. The contestants try to guess the identity of the guest. Students may enjoy assisting you in creating rules and procedures for the game.

7. Divide your class into two teams. Use *The Importance of Being Earnest* crossword words with their letters jumbled as a word list. Student 1 from Team A faces off against Student 1 from Team B. You write the first jumbled word on the board. The first student (1A or 1B) to unscramble the word wins the chance for his or her team to score points. If 1A wins the jumble, go to student 2A, and give him or her a clue. The student must give you the correct word that matches the clue. If he or she does, Team A scores a point, and you give student 3A a clue for which you expect another correct response. Continue giving Team A clues until some team member makes an incorrect response. An incorrect response sends the game back to the jumbled-word face off, this time with students 2A and 2B. Instead of repeating giving clues to the first few students of each team, continue with the student after the one who gave the last incorrect response on the team. For example, if Team B wins the jumbled-word face-off, and student 5B gave the last incorrect answer for Team B, you would start this round of clue questions with student 6B, and so on. The team with the most points wins!

8. Play Jeopardy. Divide the class into two groups. Assign each group a category from the story and have them devise answers for that category. Play the game according to the television show procedures.

9. Play Drawing in the Details. Divide students into teams. A student from one team draws a scene from the story. (You may want to specify the Act.) Drawings should be kept simple, to keep the pace lively. Students on the opposing team locate the scene in their books and read it aloud. If they are incorrect, the illustrator's team has a chance to guess. Involve students in setting up a scoring system and any other necessary rules.

LESSON SEVENTEEN

Objectives:

1. To test students' understanding of the main ideas and themes in *The Importance of Being Earnest*

Activity 1:

Distribute the unit tests. Go over the instructions in detail, and allow the students the entire class period to complete the exam.

Notes about the Unit Tests in this Unit:

There are five different unit tests included in the LitPlan Teacher Pack. Two are short answer, and two are multiple-choice. There is one advanced short answer test. The answers to the advanced short answer test will be based on the discussions you have had during class and should be graded accordingly. You should choose the tests and/or test parts that best suit your needs. Matching and short answer tests have answer keys. For essay type questions, grade according to your own criteria, based on class discussions and the level of your students. In addition, you will need to choose vocabulary words to read orally for the vocabulary section of the short answer tests.

Activity 2:

Collect all test papers and assigned books prior to the end of the class period.

UNIT TESTS

The Importance of Being Earnest - SHORT ANSWER UNIT TEST 1

I. Matching

____ 1. CECILY A. The instrument Algernon plays

____ 2. JACK B. The location of Jack's country house

____ 3. ALGERNON C. The city in which Ernest dies from a severe chill

____ 4. PRISM D. Algernon's last name

____ 5. BRACKNELL E. The sandwiches Algernon made for his aunt's visit

____ 6. MONCRIEFF F. Where Cecily and Gwendolen record their thoughts

____ 7. WORTHING G. Cecily's governess: Miss _____

____ 8. CUCUMBER H. The line of the station where the baby was found

____ 9. WOOLTON I. Gwendolen's cousin

____ 10. BRIGHTON J. The boy Mr. Thomas Cardew adopted

____ 11. PIANO K. Gwendolen's father: Lord _____

____ 12. BUNBURY L. Algernon's fictitious friend

____ 13. DIARY M. What Miss Prism accidentally swapped with the baby

____ 14. PARIS N. The Sussex resort to which Mr. Thomas Cardew was traveling

____ 15. MANUSCRIPT O. The name of Jack's ward

II. Short Answer

1. What is a "Bunburyist," and how was that label created?

2. Why does Algernon believe that the cigarette case does not belong to Jack?

3. Why does Gwendolen say she was "far from indifferent" to Jack before she met him?

4. According to Cecily, what is the main difference between events that are recorded in a diary and those recorded in memory?

5. Why was Miss Prism's novel never published?

6. How do Gwendolen and Cecily attempt to prove who is engaged to Ernest?

7. How is the conflict between Gwendolen and Cecily resolved?

8. How does Lady Bracknell respond to Algernon's news of Bunbury's death?

9. What was the unfortunate switch that Miss Prism made? What was the result?

10. What is Jack's real name, and how is that fact revealed?

III. Quotations

Explain the importance and meaning of the following quotations:

1. When one is in town one amuses oneself. When one is in the country one amuses other people.

2. We live, as I hope you know...in an age of ideals. The fact is constantly mentioned in the more expensive monthly magazines, and has reached the provincial pulpits, I am told: and my ideal has always been to love some one of the name of Ernest. There is something in that name that inspires absolute confidence.

3. I am not in favour of this modern mania for turning bad people into good people at a moment's notice. As a man sows so let him reap.

4. And you do not seem to realise, dear Doctor, that by persistently remaining single, a man converts himself into a permanent public temptation. Men should be more careful; this very celibacy leads weaker vessels astray....No married man is ever attractive except to his wife.

5. You must not laugh at me, darling, but it had always been a girlish dream of mine to love some one whose name was Ernest. There is something in that name that seems to inspire absolute confidence. I pity any poor married woman whose husband is not called Ernest.

IV. Composition

1. One of the literary techniques that is frequently utilized by Oscar Wilde is punning. In a well-organized essay, identify uses of puns in the play, and explain why they are used. Be sure to take character development, the ridicule and subversion of Victorian conventions, and the expression of uncommon views into consideration.

V. Vocabulary

Write the vocabulary words you are given. After writing them down, go back and write in their definitions.

Word	Definition
1	
2	
3	
4	
5	
6	
7	
8	
9	
10	

The Importance of Being Earnest - SHORT ANSWER UNIT TEST 1 ANSWER KEY

I. Matching

O	1. CECILY	A.	The instrument Algernon plays
J	2. JACK	B.	The location of Jack's country house
I	3. ALGERNON	C.	The city in which Ernest dies from a severe chill
G	4. PRISM	D.	Algernon's last name
K	5. BRACKNELL	E.	The sandwiches Algernon made for his aunt's visit
D	6. MONCRIEFF	F.	Where Cecily and Gwendolen record their thoughts
N	7. WORTHING	G.	Cecily's governess: Miss _____
E	8. CUCUMBER	H.	The line of the station where the baby was found
B	9. WOOLTON	I.	Gwendolen's cousin
H	10. BRIGHTON	J.	The boy Mr. Thomas Cardew adopted
A	11. PIANO	K.	Gwendolen's father: Lord _____
L	12. BUNBURY	L.	Algernon's fictitious friend
F	13. DIARY	M.	What Miss Prism accidentally swapped with the baby
C	14. PARIS	N.	The Sussex resort to which Mr. Thomas Cardew was traveling
M	15. MANUSCRIPT	O.	The name of Jack's ward

II. Short Answer

1. What is a "Bunburyist," and how was that label created?
   A Bunburyist is an individual who creates a fictitious relative or friend who requires constant care and attention. An individual may pretend to visit the friend or relative at a moment's notice, thereby having an excuse to avoid other engagements.
   The term "Bunburyist" is derived from the name of Algernon's fictitious friend, Mr. Bunbury, a sickly invalid whom Algernon visits in the country.

2. Why does Algernon believe that the cigarette case does not belong to Jack?
   Jack has never mentioned Cecily before, and Algernon does not believe Jack is acquainted with anyone by that name. Additionally, Algernon refuses to believe Jack's story that Cecily is his aunt, especially since the person who wrote the inscription describes herself as "little" and addresses him as "Uncle Jack." Finally, Jack had Algernon convinced that his name is Ernest. Jack later explains that he goes by the name Jack in the country and Ernest in the city.

3. Why does Gwendolen say she was "far from indifferent" to Jack before she met him?
   Gwendolen has always wanted to love someone named Ernest, and when Algernon mentioned to her that he had a friend by that name, she thought that she was destined to fall in love with him.

4. According to Cecily, what is the main difference between events that are recorded in a diary and those recorded in memory?
   The events that are recorded in a diary are truthful and accurate; those that are recorded in memory are fictitious, just like those in novels.

5. Why was Miss Prism's novel never published?
   Miss Prism's novel was lost, and, as a result, it could not be published.

6. How do Gwendolen and Cecily attempt to prove who is engaged to Ernest?
   Each woman argues that her engagement is valid because it will soon be published in the local newspaper. Additionally, each has written about the proposal in her diary. Ernest's proposal to Cecily took place ten minutes prior to her conversation with Gwendolen, and his proposal to Gwendolen took place at 5:30 p.m. the previous day.

7. How is the conflict between Gwendolen and Cecily resolved?
   Cecily reveals that the man Gwendolen is engaged to is really her guardian, Jack Worthing. Gwendolen, in a similar fashion, says that Cecily's fiancé is her cousin, Algernon Moncrieff. Once the two women discover that they have been deceived, they unite and turn against the men.

8. How does Lady Bracknell respond to Algernon's news of Bunbury's death?
   Lady Bracknell is happy that Bunbury is dead. She is glad that he finally "made up his mind at the last to some definite course of action."

9. What was the unfortunate switch that Miss Prism made? What was the result?
   Miss Prism accidentally put the baby she was watching in her hand-bag and her manuscript in the baby carriage. Miss Prism then accidentally left the hand-bag in the cloak-room of Victoria Station.

10. What is Jack's real name, and how is that fact revealed?
    Jack's real name is Ernest. His father was a General, and his name could be found in the Army List. When Jack looks up the name, he discovers that his father's name was Ernest. Because Jack is the eldest son, he is named after his father.

The Importance of Being Earnest - SHORT ANSWER UNIT TEST 2

I. Matching

____ 1. ERNEST   A. Jack's fiancée

____ 2. GWENDOLEN   B. The name of Jack's fictitious brother

____ 3. AUGUSTA   C. Cecily's last name

____ 4. MUFFINS   D. The club to which Algernon and Jack belong

____ 5. CARDEW   E. The baby was discovered in a _____

____ 6. VICTORIA   F. Lady Bracknell's first name

____ 7. HANDBAG   G. The train station where the baby was found

____ 8. DIARY   H. Where Cecily and Gwendolen record their thoughts

____ 9. EMPIRE   I. The baked good that Algernon enjoys eating

____ 10. GENERAL   J. Jack's father's title in the army

II. Short Answer

1. Why does Algernon believe marriage proposals are unromantic?

2. Why did Jack create Ernest, his alter ego?

3. Who is Cecily Cardew, and how is she connected to Jack?

4. How did Jack come to live with Mr. Thomas Cardew and his family?

5. How do Lady Bracknell's views on marriage differ from Gwendolen's?

6. Why does Jack arrive at his country house dressed in all black?

7. What does Cecily mean when she says that she and Ernest have been engaged for three months?

8. What is the cause of the confusion between Gwendolen and Cecily?

9. Who is the baby that Miss Prism lost? How is this fact proven?

10. What is revealed to be the relationship between Algernon and Jack?

III. Quotations

Explain the importance and meaning of the following quotations:

1. I really don't see anything romantic in proposing. It is very romantic to be in love. But there is nothing romantic about a definite proposal. Why, one may be accepted. One usually is, I believe. Then the excitement is all over. The very essence of romance is uncertainty. If ever I get married, I'll certainly try to forget the fact.

2. Oh! it is absurd to have a hard-and-fast rule about what one should read and what one shouldn't. More than half of modern culture depends on what one shouldn't read.

3. You have always told me [your name] was Ernest. I have introduced you to everyone as Ernest. You answer to the name of Ernest. You look as if your name was Ernest. You are the most earnest-looking person I ever saw in my life. It is perfectly absurd your saying that your name isn't Ernest. It's on your cards.

4. Ernest has a strong upright nature. He is the very soul of truth and honour. Disloyalty would be as impossible to him as deception. But even men of the noblest possible moral character are extremely susceptible to the influence of the physical charms of others. Modern, no less than Ancient History, supplies us with many most painful examples of what I refer to. If it were not so, indeed, History would be unreadable.

5. I never travel without my diary. On should always have something sensational to read in the train.

IV. Composition

1. At the beginning of the play, Algernon says to Lane, "I don't play accurately...any one can play accurately...but I play with wonderful expression. As far as the piano is concerned, sentiment is my forte. I keep science for Life." What can you infer about Algernon's character by this statement, and how do the values and beliefs expressed explain his behavior in the play?

2. Do you feel satisfied with the ending of the play? Are the revelation and the new character relationships it creates realistic? Is the ending foreshadowed, or does it seem unexpected? Is it realistic or contrived? Develop your ideas into a well-organized essay.

V. Vocabulary

Write the vocabulary words you are given. After writing them down, go back and write in their definitions.

Word	Definition
1	
2	
3	
4	
5	
6	
7	
8	
9	
10	

The Importance of Being Earnest - SHORT ANSWER UNIT TEST 2 ANSWER KEY

I. Matching

B	1.	ERNEST	A.	Jack's fiancée
A	2.	GWENDOLEN	B.	The name of Jack's fictitious brother
F	3.	AUGUSTA	C.	Cecily's last name
I	4.	MUFFINS	D.	The club to which Algernon and Jack belong
C	5.	CARDEW	E.	The baby was discovered in a _____
G	6.	VICTORIA	F.	Lady Bracknell's first name
E	7.	HANDBAG	G.	The train station where the baby was found
H	8.	DIARY	H.	Where Cecily and Gwendolen record their thoughts
D	9.	EMPIRE	I.	The baked good that Algernon enjoys eating
J	10.	GENERAL	J.	Jack's father's title in the army

II. Short Answer

1. Why does Algernon believe marriage proposals are unromantic?
   Algernon feels that love is romantic only when it is uncertain. Once the proposal is accepted, the excitement is over. Love ceases to be uncertain and, therefore, becomes unromantic.
2. Why did Jack create Ernest, his alter ego?
   Ever since Jack became Cecily's guardian, he has been forced to act morally in order to set a good example for her. However, Jack is not moral and upright by nature, and he feels that he needs to escape from home to be himself. For this reason, he has told his friends in the country that he has a younger brother named Ernest in the Albany, who is always getting into trouble. When Jack goes to "visit" Ernest, he actual goes to the city.
3. Who is Cecily Cardew, and how is she connected to Jack?
   Cecily Cardew is Jack's ward. She lives at Jack's country house with a governess, Miss Prism. Cecily's grandfather, Thomas Cardew, adopted Jack when he was a boy and, later, made Jack Cecily's legal guardian. Even though she is not related to Jack, Cecily respectfully calls him uncle.
4. How did Jack come to live with Mr. Thomas Cardew and his family?
   Mr. Thomas Cardew found Jack in a hand-bag in the cloak-room of Victoria Station. Cardew adopted Jack and made him a member of his family, giving him the surname Worthing after the name of the resort he was traveling to when he found him.
5. How do Lady Bracknell's views on marriage differ from Gwendolen's?
   Lady Bracknell believes that a marriage should be arranged by a young woman's parents. The mother of the future bride should choose the most eligible bachelor to be her daughter's husband. The daughter should not be allowed to choose her husband herself.
6. Why does Jack arrive at his country house dressed in all black?
   Jack is dressed in black because he wants his friends in the country to believe that he is in mourning. Jack is carrying out his plan to eliminate his imaginary brother Ernest. He tells Miss Prism and Dr. Chasuble that he received a telegram the previous evening from the manager of the Grand Hotel in Paris; Ernest had died of a severe chill, and his body is going to be buried in Paris.
7. What does Cecily mean when she says that she and Ernest have been engaged for three months?
   Cecily fell in love with Ernest after hearing Jack talk about him and his bad behavior. She imagined that he proposed to her under the old tree on February 14th. She bought herself a ring from Ernest, and she started wearing a bracelet with a lover's knot that she promised to never take off. In addition, Cecily wrote letters to herself from Ernest. She broke off the imaginary engagement on March 22nd, because she believes that all serious engagements have to be broken off at least once. By the following week, however, the engagement was resumed.
8. What is the cause of the confusion between Gwendolen and Cecily?
   Gwendolen and Cecily are both engaged to Ernest, even though he does not exist. In reality, Gwendolen is engaged to Jack Worthing, who calls himself Ernest in the city, and Cecily is engaged to Algernon Moncrieff, who is pretending to be Jack's fictitious brother Ernest.
9. Who is the baby that Miss Prism lost? How is this fact proven?
   Jack is the baby whom Miss Prism lost. This fact is proven when he shows Miss Prism with the hand-bag, which she identifies as her own.
10. What is revealed to be the relationship between Algernon and Jack?
    Jack and Algernon are brothers.

The Importance of Being Earnest - MULTIPLE-CHOICE UNIT TEST 1

I. Matching

____ 1.   ERNEST   A. The baked good that Algernon enjoys eating

____ 2.   GWENDOLEN   B. The name of Jack's fictitious brother

____ 3.   AUGUSTA   C. The baby was discovered in a _____

____ 4.   MUFFINS   D. Where Cecily and Gwendolen record their thoughts

____ 5.   CARDEW   E. Jack's father's title in the army

____ 6.   VICTORIA   F. Cecily's last name

____ 7.   HANDBAG   G. Lady Bracknell's first name

____ 8.   DIARY   H. The train station where the baby was found

____ 9.   EMPIRE   I. The club to which Algernon and Jack belong

____ 10. GENERAL   J. Jack's fiancée

II. Multiple-Choice

1. Which is NOT a reason Algernon believes the cigarette case does not belong to Jack?
    A. Jack is known to everyone in the city as Ernest.
    B. Jack prefers snuff to cigarettes or cigars.
    C. Jack has never mentioned anyone named Cecily.
    D. Jack's aunt would not refer to him as "Uncle Jack."

2. Why did Jack create Ernest, his alter ego?
    A. Jack could not handle the pressure to always act morally.
    B. Jack did not want Cecily to know about Gwendolen.
    C. Jack wanted the freedom to travel to Paris on a whim.
    D. Jack wanted to escape the shallowness of city life.

3. How did Jack come to live with Mr. Thomas Cardew and his family?
    A. Mr. Thomas Cardew found Jack in a hand-bag in the cloak-room at Victoria Station.
    B. Jack's parents could not afford to raise him and gave him up for adoption.
    C. Mr. Thomas Cardew rescued Jack from the streets after his parents disowned him.
    D. Mr. Thomas Cardew adopted Jack when his parents were killed in an accident.

4. Why is Gwendolen critical of Jack's marriage proposal?
    A. It appears that Jack has not practiced proposing.
    B. She knows Lady Bracknell would never approve.
    C. Jack is not in the financial situation to consider marrying.
    D. Jack knows that Gwendolen is in love with Algernon.

5. According to Cecily, what is the main difference between events that are recorded in a diary and those recorded in memory?
    A. The events in a diary are extraordinary; those in memory are commonplace.
    B. The events in a diary are interesting; those in memory are boring.
    C. The events in a diary are significant; those in memory are unimportant.
    D. The events in a diary are true; those in memory are fictitious.

6. How has Cecily been engaged to Ernest for three months?
    A. Jack pretended to be Ernest, and wrote a letter proposing to Cecily.
    B. Ernest and Cecily secretly became engaged in Paris.
    C. Algernon drunkenly proposed to Cecily at Jack's city house.
    D. Cecily imagined that Ernest proposed to her three months earlier.

7. How do Gwendolen and Cecily attempt to prove who is really engaged to Ernest?
    A. They ask Miss Prism and Lady Bracknell who Ernest truly loves.
    B. They ask Ernest which one of them he is going to marry.
    C. They use their diaries to prove when they became engaged to Ernest.
    D. They show each other the love letters that Ernest wrote them.

8. In Act II, what do Algernon and Jack do after the women leave the room?
   A. They go to the rectory to be christened.
   B. They go to dinner at the Empire Club.
   C. They argue with each other while eating muffins.
   D. They go to the city to visit Mr. Bunbury.

9. How does Lady Bracknell know Miss Prism?
   A. Miss Prism is Algernon's mother.
   B. Miss Prism once worked for Lady Bracknell.
   C. Miss Prism was Algernon's nurse.
   D. Miss Prism is Lady Bracknell's sister.

10. How is it determined that Jack's birth name is Ernest?
    A. Jack's birth certificate is found within the pages of Miss Prism's manuscript.
    B. Dr. Chasuble knows the rector who christened Jack when he was a baby.
    C. Jack was named after his father, whose name was Ernest.
    D. Lady Bracknell recorded Jack's real birth name in her diary.

III. Quotations

Explain the importance and meaning of the following quotations:

1. When one is in town one amuses oneself. When one is in the country one amuses other people.

2. We live, as I hope you know...in an age of ideals. The fact is constantly mentioned in the more expensive monthly magazines, and has reached the provincial pulpits, I am told: and my ideal has always been to love some one of the name of Ernest. There is something in that name that inspires absolute confidence.

3. I am not in favour of this modern mania for turning bad people into good people at a moment's notice. As a man sows so let him reap.

4. And you do not seem to realise, dear Doctor, that by persistently remaining single, a man converts himself into a permanent public temptation. Men should be more careful; this very celibacy leads weaker vessels astray....No married man is ever attractive except to his wife.

5. You must not laugh at me, darling, but it had always been a girlish dream of mine to love some one whose name was Ernest. There is something in that name that seems to inspire absolute confidence. I pity any poor married woman whose husband is not called Ernest.

IV. Composition

1. Compare and contrast Algernon's Bunburying and Jack's visiting his fictitious brother Ernest. Why does each character deceive his friends and family members, and how do the differences in their reasons establish the characters as foils?

2. In Act III, what does the exchange between Lady Bracknell and Jack, in which they discuss Cecily's background, suggest about marriage and match-making in the Victorian Era?

V. Vocabulary

____ 1. CANDIDLY   A. seriousness; coldness

____ 2. PROPOUNDING   B. unable to be bypassed or overlooked

____ 3. DEMONSTRATIVE   C. a deception or false claim

____ 4. METAPHYSICAL   D. depressing or spiritless

____ 5. INDECOROUS   E. calmness and composure

____ 6. DISPOSITION   F. rudeness or shamelessness

____ 7. GRAVITY   G. abstract and philosophical

____ 8. VACILLATING   H. improper; unmannerly

____ 9. QUIXOTIC   I. given in abundance

____ 10. MELANCHOLY   J. expressive or affectionate

____ 11. EQUANIMITY   K. can be passed from an individual to his or her offspring

____ 12. PHILANTHROPIC   L. done beforehand or in preparation for

____ 13. HEREDITARY   M. indecisive or wavering

____ 14. EFFRONTERY   N. truthfully and sincerely

____ 15. INSUPERABLE   O. having to do with the giving of money or services to help others

____ 16. PRELIMINARY   P. putting forth for others to consider

____ 17. OSTENTATIOUSLY   Q. dreamy, romantic, and idealistic

____ 18. PRETENSE   R. spacious or having the ability to hold a lot

____ 19. CAPACIOUS   S. in a showy manner; extravagantly

____ 20. LAVISHED   T. a person's behavior and attitude

The Importance of Being Earnest - MULTIPLE-CHOICE UNIT TEST 1 ANSWER KEY

I. Matching

B	1.	ERNEST	A.	The baked good that Algernon enjoys eating
J	2.	GWENDOLEN	B.	The name of Jack's fictitious brother
G	3.	AUGUSTA	C.	The baby was discovered in a _____
A	4.	MUFFINS	D.	Where Cecily and Gwendolen record their thoughts
F	5.	CARDEW	E.	Jack's father's title in the army
H	6.	VICTORIA	F.	Cecily's last name
C	7.	HANDBAG	G.	Lady Bracknell's first name
D	8.	DIARY	H.	The train station where the baby was found
I	9.	EMPIRE	I.	The club to which Algernon and Jack belong
E	10.	GENERAL	J.	Jack's fiancée

II. Multiple-Choice

B 1. Which is NOT a reason Algernon believes the cigarette case does not belong to Jack?
   A. Jack is known to everyone in the city as Ernest.
   B. Jack prefers snuff to cigarettes or cigars.
   C. Jack has never mentioned anyone named Cecily.
   D. Jack's aunt would not refer to him as "Uncle Jack."

A 2. Why did Jack create Ernest, his alter ego?
   A. Jack could not handle the pressure to always act morally.
   B. Jack did not want Cecily to know about Gwendolen.
   C. Jack wanted the freedom to travel to Paris on a whim.
   D. Jack wanted to escape the shallowness of city life.

A 3. How did Jack come to live with Mr. Thomas Cardew and his family?
   A. Mr. Thomas Cardew found Jack in a hand-bag in the cloak-room at Victoria Station.
   B. Jack's parents could not afford to raise him and gave him up for adoption.
   C. Mr. Thomas Cardew rescued Jack from the streets after his parents disowned him.
   D. Mr. Thomas Cardew adopted Jack when his parents were killed in an accident.

A 4. Why is Gwendolen critical of Jack's marriage proposal?
   A. It appears that Jack has not practiced proposing.
   B. She knows Lady Bracknell would never approve.
   C. Jack is not in the financial situation to consider marrying.
   D. Jack knows that Gwendolen is in love with Algernon.

D 5. According to Cecily, what is the main difference between events that are recorded in a diary and those recorded in memory?
   A. The events in a diary are extraordinary; those in memory are commonplace.
   B. The events in a diary are interesting; those in memory are boring.
   C. The events in a diary are significant; those in memory are unimportant.
   D. The events in a diary are true; those in memory are fictitious.

D 6. How has Cecily been engaged to Ernest for three months?
   A. Jack pretended to be Ernest, and wrote a letter proposing to Cecily.
   B. Ernest and Cecily secretly became engaged in Paris.
   C. Algernon drunkenly proposed to Cecily at Jack's city house.
   D. Cecily imagined that Ernest proposed to her three months earlier.

C 7. How do Gwendolen and Cecily attempt to prove who is really engaged to Ernest?
   A. They ask Miss Prism and Lady Bracknell who Ernest truly loves.
   B. They ask Ernest which one of them he is going to marry.
   C. They use their diaries to prove when they became engaged to Ernest.
   D. They show each other the love letters that Ernest wrote them.

C 8. In Act II, what do Algernon and Jack do after the women leave the room?
   A. They go to the rectory to be christened.
   B. They go to dinner at the Empire Club.
   C. They argue with each other while eating muffins.
   D. They go to the city to visit Mr. Bunbury.

B 9. How does Lady Bracknell know Miss Prism?
   A. Miss Prism is Algernon's mother.
   B. Miss Prism once worked for Lady Bracknell.
   C. Miss Prism was Algernon's nurse.
   D. Miss Prism is Lady Bracknell's sister.

C 10. How is it determined that Jack's birth name is Ernest?
   A. Jack's birth certificate is found within the pages of Miss Prism's manuscript.
   B. Dr. Chasuble knows the rector who christened Jack when he was a baby.
   C. Jack was named after his father, whose name was Ernest.
   D. Lady Bracknell recorded Jack's real birth name in her diary.

V. Vocabulary

N	1.	CANDIDLY	A. seriousness; coldness
P	2.	PROPOUNDING	B. unable to be bypassed or overlooked
J	3.	DEMONSTRATIVE	C. a deception or false claim
G	4.	METAPHYSICAL	D. depressing or spiritless
H	5.	INDECOROUS	E. calmness and composure
T	6.	DISPOSITION	F. rudeness or shamelessness
A	7.	GRAVITY	G. abstract and philosophical
M	8.	VACILLATING	H. improper; unmannerly
Q	9.	QUIXOTIC	I. given in abundance
D	10.	MELANCHOLY	J. expressive or affectionate
E	11.	EQUANIMITY	K. can be passed from an individual to his or her offspring
O	12.	PHILANTHROPIC	L. done beforehand or in preparation for
K	13.	HEREDITARY	M. indecisive or wavering
F	14.	EFFRONTERY	N. truthfully and sincerely
B	15.	INSUPERABLE	O. having to do with the giving of money or services to help others
L	16.	PRELIMINARY	P. putting forth for others to consider
S	17.	OSTENTATIOUSLY	Q. dreamy, romantic, and idealistic
C	18.	PRETENSE	R. spacious or having the ability to hold a lot
R	19.	CAPACIOUS	S. in a showy manner; extravagantly
I	20.	LAVISHED	T. a person's behavior and attitude

The Importance of Being Earnest - MULTIPLE-CHOICE UNIT TEST 2

I. Matching

____ 1. CECILY   A. The city in which Ernest dies from a severe chill

____ 2. JACK   B. Algernon's fictitious friend

____ 3. ALGERNON   C. Gwendolen's cousin

____ 4. PRISM   D. Cecily's governess: Miss _____

____ 5. BRACKNELL   E. The sandwiches Algernon made for his aunt's visit

____ 6. MONCRIEFF   F. The location of Jack's country house

____ 7. WORTHING   G. Gwendolen's father: Lord _____

____ 8. CUCUMBER   H. The line of the station where the baby was found

____ 9. WOOLTON   I. The instrument Algernon plays

____ 10. BRIGHTON   J. What Miss Prism accidentally swapped with the baby

____ 11. PIANO   K. Where Cecily and Gwendolen record their thoughts

____ 12. BUNBURY   L. The name of Jack's ward

____ 13. DIARY   M. The Sussex resort to which Mr. Thomas Cardew was traveling

____ 14. PARIS   N. Algernon's last name

____ 15. MANUSCRIPT   O. The boy Mr. Thomas Cardew adopted

II. Multiple-Choice

1. What is a "Bunburyist"?
   A. a person who lives in both the city and the country
   B. someone who frequently leaves home to visit a fictitious person
   C. a widower who marries a woman less than half his age
   D. a person who requires constant medical care and supervision

2. What is the inscription on the cigarette case?
   A. "From little Cecily, with her fondest love to her dear Uncle Jack."
   B. "From little Gwendolen, with her fondest love to her dear Uncle Ernest."
   C. "From little Gwendolen, with her fondest love to her dear Uncle Jack."
   D. "From little Cecily, with her fondest love to her dear Uncle Ernest."

3. Why does Gwendolen say she was "far from indifferent" to Jack before she met him?
   A. She started to love him when she heard about his kindness and generosity.
   B. Algernon told her Jack would be superior to her other suitors.
   C. She started to love him when she learned that his name is Ernest.
   D. She knew he was very rich and popular in high society.

4. How does Lady Bracknell believe engagements should be made?
   A. A young woman's parents should choose a husband for her.
   B. A young woman's parents should buy her husband with a dowry.
   C. A young woman should marry the wealthiest man she knows.
   D. A young woman should accept the proposal of the man she loves.

5. Why was Miss Prism's novel never published?
   A. Her manuscript was destroyed by Lady Bracknell.
   B. Her manuscript was lost before it was published.
   C. The publishers thought her novel was too scandalous.
   D. The publishers thought her novel was uninteresting.

6. Why does Miss Prism believe it not a good idea to try to reform bad men?
   A. Bad men amplify the virtues of those who are good by sharp contrast.
   B. Men should sow what they reap and be responsible for their actions.
   C. Men are predestined to be who they are by the will of God.
   D. Bad men make conversations more lively and interesting.

7. What favor does Jack ask of Dr. Chasuble?
   A. to marry him and Gwendolen that night
   B. to christen Algernon
   C. to reveal the identities of his birth parents
   D. to christen him

8. How does Lady Bracknell respond to Algernon's news of Bunbury's death?
   A. She is furious that Bunbury chose to die at such an unfortunate time.
   B. She feels sorry for her nephew, who is grieving over his friend's death.
   C. She is happy that Bunbury finally decided whether he wanted to live or die.
   D. She worries that Bunbury's death was caused by a typhus epidemic.

9. Which of the following is NOT something Jack says to get Lady Bracknell to approve of Algernon's marriage to Cecily?
    A. Cecily is the granddaughter of a French baroness.
    B. Cecily's family's solicitors are Messrs. Markby, Markby, and Markby.
    C. Cecily has one hundred and thirty thousand pounds in funds.
    D. Cecily's grandfather, Mr. Thomas Cardew, owned three homes.

10. How is it determined that Jack's birth name is Ernest?
    A. Lady Bracknell recorded Jack's real birth name in her diary.
    B. Dr. Chasuble knows the rector who christened Jack when he was a baby.
    C. Jack's birth certificate is found within the pages of Miss Prism's manuscript.
    D. Jack was named after his father, whose name was Ernest.

III. Quotations

Explain the importance and meaning of the following quotations:

1. I really don't see anything romantic in proposing. It is very romantic to be in love. But there is nothing romantic about a definite proposal. Why, one may be accepted. One usually is, I believe. Then the excitement is all over. The very essence of romance is uncertainty. If ever I get married, I'll certainly try to forget the fact.

2. Oh! it is absurd to have a hard-and-fast rule about what one should read and what one shouldn't. More than half of modern culture depends on what one shouldn't read.

3. You have always told me [your name] was Ernest. I have introduced you to everyone as Ernest. You answer to the name of Ernest. You look as if your name was Ernest. You are the most earnest-looking person I ever saw in my life. It is perfectly absurd your saying that your name isn't Ernest. It's on your cards.

4. Ernest, we may never be married. From the expression on mamma's face I fear we never shall. Few parents now-a-days pay any regard to what their children say to them. The old-fashioned respect for the young is fast dying out. Whatever influence I ever had over mamma, I lost at the age of three. But although she may prevent us from becoming man and wife, and I may marry someone else, and marry often, nothing that she can possibly do can alter my eternal devotion to you.

5. I never travel without my diary. On should always have something sensational to read in the train.

IV. Composition

1. Before the cigarette case interrogation scene, Algernon seems to know that the case belongs to Jack. If Algernon had merely given Jack the case without asking questions, how would this play have been different?

2. In Act II, what does writing...in the form of diary entries, letters, and manuscripts...suggest about the importance of the written word and the nature of history?

V. Vocabulary

____ 1. SENTENTIOUSLY A. relating to usefulness instead of grace, beauty, or sophistication

____ 2. CYNICAL B. overly fond of and permissive

____ 3. GLIBLY C. something unimportant and superficial

____ 4. SOLITUDE D. an expression of regret for doing something wrong

____ 5. COMMERCE E. the state of being alone; seclusion

____ 6. UTILITARIAN F. rash and careless

____ 7. TRIVIALITY G. bitter and distrustful

____ 8. MELODRAMATIC H. schemes or tricks

____ 9. MISANTHROPE I. disgusted or annoyed

____ 10. GROTESQUE J. unnatural, bizarre, and hideous

____ 11. IMPETUOUS K. believability; inspiring trust and faith in an idea

____ 12. MACHINATIONS L. an individual who hates people

____ 13. REPENTANCE M. informed; given knowledge of

____ 14. CREDULITY N. to cringe with fear

____ 15. APPRISED O. sobriety; abstaining from drinking alcohol

____ 16. MERCENARY P. providing a service only for financial gain

____ 17. INDIGNANT Q. relating to trade or business

____ 18. QUAIL R. self-righteously; expressing wise sayings and aphorisms

____ 19. TEMPERANCE S. overemotional and theatrical

____ 20. DOTING T. spoken flippantly or without prior thought

The Importance of Being Earnest - MULTIPLE-CHOICE UNIT TEST 2 ANSWER KEY

I. Matching

L	1. CECILY		A.	The city in which Ernest dies from a severe chill
O	2. JACK		B.	Algernon's fictitious friend
C	3. ALGERNON		C.	Gwendolen's cousin
D	4. PRISM		D.	Cecily's governess: Miss _____
G	5. BRACKNELL		E.	The sandwiches Algernon made for his aunt's visit
N	6. MONCRIEFF		F.	The location of Jack's country house
M	7. WORTHING		G.	Gwendolen's father: Lord _____
E	8. CUCUMBER		H.	The line of the station where the baby was found
F	9. WOOLTON		I.	The instrument Algernon plays
H	10. BRIGHTON		J.	What Miss Prism accidentally swapped with the baby
I	11. PIANO		K.	Where Cecily and Gwendolen record their thoughts
B	12. BUNBURY		L.	The name of Jack's ward
K	13. DIARY		M.	The Sussex resort to which Mr. Thomas Cardew was traveling
A	14. PARIS		N.	Algernon's last name
J	15. MANUSCRIPT		O.	The boy Mr. Thomas Cardew adopted

II. Multiple-Choice

B 1. What is a "Bunburyist"?
   A. a person who lives in both the city and the country
   B. someone who frequently leaves home to visit a fictitious person
   C. a widower who marries a woman less than half his age
   D. a person who requires constant medical care and supervision

A 2. What is the inscription on the cigarette case?
   A. "From little Cecily, with her fondest love to her dear Uncle Jack."
   B. "From little Gwendolen, with her fondest love to her dear Uncle Ernest."
   C. "From little Gwendolen, with her fondest love to her dear Uncle Jack."
   D. "From little Cecily, with her fondest love to her dear Uncle Ernest."

C 3. Why does Gwendolen say she was "far from indifferent" to Jack before she met him?
   A. She started to love him when she heard about his kindness and generosity.
   B. Algernon told her Jack would be superior to her other suitors.
   C. She started to love him when she learned that his name is Ernest.
   D. She knew he was very rich and popular in high society.

A 4. How does Lady Bracknell believe engagements should be made?
   A. A young woman's parents should choose a husband for her.
   B. A young woman's parents should buy her husband with a dowry.
   C. A young woman should marry the wealthiest man she knows.
   D. A young woman should accept the proposal of the man she loves.

B 5. Why was Miss Prism's novel never published?
   A. Her manuscript was destroyed by Lady Bracknell.
   B. Her manuscript was lost before it was published.
   C. The publishers thought her novel was too scandalous.
   D. The publishers thought her novel was uninteresting.

B 6. Why does Miss Prism believe it not a good idea to try to reform bad men?
   A. Bad men amplify the virtues of those who are good by sharp contrast.
   B. Men should sow what they reap and be responsible for their actions.
   C. Men are predestined to be who they are by the will of God.
   D. Bad men make conversations more lively and interesting.

D 7. What favor does Jack ask of Dr. Chasuble?
   A. to marry him and Gwendolen that night
   B. to christen Algernon
   C. to reveal the identities of his birth parents
   D. to christen him

C 8. How does Lady Bracknell respond to Algernon's news of Bunbury's death?
   A. She is furious that Bunbury chose to die at such an unfortunate time.
   B. She feels sorry for her nephew, who is grieving over his friend's death.
   C. She is happy that Bunbury finally decided whether he wanted to live or die.
   D. She worries that Bunbury's death was caused by a typhus epidemic.

A 9. Which of the following is NOT something Jack says to get Lady Bracknell to approve of Algernon's marriage to Cecily?
   A. Cecily is the granddaughter of a French baroness.
   B. Cecily's family's solicitors are Messrs. Markby, Markby, and Markby.
   C. Cecily has one hundred and thirty thousand pounds in funds.
   D. Cecily's grandfather, Mr. Thomas Cardew, owned three homes.

D 10. How is it determined that Jack's birth name is Ernest?
   A. Lady Bracknell recorded Jack's real birth name in her diary.
   B. Dr. Chasuble knows the rector who christened Jack when he was a baby.
   C. Jack's birth certificate is found within the pages of Miss Prism's manuscript.
   D. Jack was named after his father, whose name was Ernest.

V. Vocabulary

R	1.	SENTENTIOUSLY	A.	relating to usefulness instead of grace, beauty, or sophistication
G	2.	CYNICAL	B.	overly fond of and permissive
T	3.	GLIBLY	C.	something unimportant and superficial
E	4.	SOLITUDE	D.	an expression of regret for doing something wrong
Q	5.	COMMERCE	E.	the state of being alone; seclusion
A	6.	UTILITARIAN	F.	rash and careless
C	7.	TRIVIALITY	G.	bitter and distrustful
S	8.	MELODRAMATIC	H.	schemes or tricks
L	9.	MISANTHROPE	I.	disgusted or annoyed
J	10.	GROTESQUE	J.	unnatural, bizarre, and hideous
F	11.	IMPETUOUS	K.	believability; inspiring trust and faith in an idea
H	12.	MACHINATIONS	L.	an individual who hates people
D	13.	REPENTANCE	M.	informed; given knowledge of
K	14.	CREDULITY	N.	to cringe with fear
M	15.	APPRISED	O.	sobriety; abstaining from drinking alcohol
P	16.	MERCENARY	P.	providing a service only for financial gain
I	17.	INDIGNANT	Q.	relating to trade or business
N	18.	QUAIL	R.	self-righteously; expressing wise sayings and aphorisms
O	19.	TEMPERANCE	S.	overemotional and theatrical
B	20.	DOTING	T.	spoken flippantly or without prior thought

The Importance of Being Earnest - ADVANCED SHORT ANSWER UNIT TEST

I. Matching

____ 1. ERNEST A. The train station where the baby was found

____ 2. JACK B. The boy Mr. Thomas Cardew adopted

____ 3. ALGERNON C. Jack's father's title in the army

____ 4. AUGUSTA D. Gwendolen's cousin

____ 5. BRACKNELL E. Where Cecily and Gwendolen record their thoughts

____ 6. WORTHING F. Lady Bracknell's first name

____ 7. VICTORIA G. The Sussex resort to which Mr. Thomas Cardew was traveling

____ 8. BUNBURY H. Algernon's fictitious friend

____ 9. DIARY I. Gwendolen's father: Lord _____

____ 10. GENERAL J. The name of Jack's fictitious brother

II. Short Answer

1. At the beginning of the play, Algernon says to Lane, "I don't play accurately...any one can play accurately...but I play with wonderful expression. As far as the piano is concerned, sentiment is my forte. I keep science for Life." What can you infer about Algernon's character by this statement, and how do the values and beliefs expressed explain his behavior in the play?

2. What seems to be the purpose of eating in this play (e.g., the cucumber sandwiches and the muffins)? Does the act of eating contribute to a theme or motif in the play? Does it indicate the emotional states of the characters? Justify your response with examples from the text.

3. Compare and contrast Algernon's Bunburying and Jack's visiting his fictitious brother Ernest. Why does each character deceive his friends and family members, and how do the differences in their reasons establish the characters as foils?

4. In Act I, several ideas about love are expressed. Identify these ideas, and explain how a conflict between them underlies the plot of the play.

5. Lady Bracknell is reluctant to allow Gwendolen to marry Jack because his parentage is uncertain: he was found in a hand-bag in Victoria Station, and there is no way to determine his social standing. In general, how is the issue of class status treated in this play? Explain your answer with examples from the text.

6. What is the view of Jack presented by Cecily? Does this validate or refute the statements he makes in Act I about his life in the country and how he presents himself to his ward?

7. In the scene where Jack arrives at the country house, ignorant of the fact that Algernon is there, how does Oscar Wilde use dramatic irony to create suspense? Additionally, does the suspense merely raise the audience's interest, or does it place emphasis on a certain scene, theme, or motif? Explain your answer.

8. In Act II, what does writing...in the form of diary entries, letters, and manuscripts...suggest about the importance of the written word and the nature of history?

9. Explain the power struggle between Cecily and Gwendolen in Act II, when they meet for the first time. How does each woman attempt to demean the other and make herself look better?

10. Are the female characters in this play (e.g., Cecily, Gwendolen, Lady Bracknell, and Miss Prism) presented as stereotypes, intentional deviations from stereotypes, or mentally and emotionally complex individuals? Use textual examples to support your answer.

III. Composition

1. One of the literary techniques that is frequently utilized by Oscar Wilde is punning. In a well-organized essay, identify uses of puns in the play, and explain why they are used. Be sure to take character development, the ridicule and subversion of Victorian conventions, and the expression of uncommon views into consideration.

2. In a well-organized essay, trace the theme of the creation, discovery, and evaluation of identity in this play.

IV. Quotations

Explain the importance and meaning of the following quotations:

1. When one is in town one amuses oneself. When one is in the country one amuses other people.

2. Well, in the first place girls never marry the men they flirt with. Girl's don't think it right....It is a great truth. It accounts for the extraordinary number of bachelors that one sees all over the place.

3. I am not in favour of this modern mania for turning bad people into good people at a moment's notice. As a man sows so let him reap.

4. I keep a diary in order to enter the wonderful secrets of my life. If I didn't write them down, I should probably forget all about them...[Memory] usually chronicles the things that have never happened, and couldn't possibly have happened. I believe that Memory is responsible for nearly all the three-volume novels that Mudie sends us.

5. Ernest has a strong upright nature. He is the very soul of truth and honour. Disloyalty would be as impossible to him as deception. But even men of the noblest possible moral character are extremely susceptible to the influence of the physical charms of others. Modern, no less than Ancient History, supplies us with many most painful examples of what I refer to. If it were not so, indeed, History would be unreadable.

V. Vocabulary

A. Write the vocabulary words you are given. After writing them down, go back and write in their definitions.

Word	Definition
1	
2	
3	
4	
5	
6	
7	
8	
9	
10	

B. Write a paragraph about the play using 8 of the 10 vocabulary words above.

The Importance of Being Earnest - ADVANCED SHORT ANSWER UNIT TEST ANSWER KEY

I. Matching

J	1. ERNEST		A.	The train station where the baby was found
B	2. JACK		B.	The boy Mr. Thomas Cardew adopted
D	3. ALGERNON		C.	Jack's father's title in the army
F	4. AUGUSTA		D.	Gwendolen's cousin
I	5. BRACKNELL		E.	Where Cecily and Gwendolen record their thoughts
G	6. WORTHING		F.	Lady Bracknell's first name
A	7. VICTORIA		G.	The Sussex resort to which Mr. Thomas Cardew was traveling
H	8. BUNBURY		H.	Algernon's fictitious friend
E	9. DIARY		I.	Gwendolen's father: Lord _____
C	10. GENERAL		J.	The name of Jack's fictitious brother

UNIT RESOURCE MATERIALS

BULLETIN BOARD IDEAS - *The Importance of Being Earnest*

1. Have students create calling cards for the characters or write messages from one character to another. Use these to decorate the bulletin board.

2. Using the lecture notes in this LitPlan or your own notes, display important information about the Victorian Era.

3. Using images of Oscar Wilde and either notes from the About the Author section or your own notes, post biographical information on Oscar Wilde or a time line of his life.

4. Divide your class into four groups, and assign each group one of the following motifs:

   • Courtship and Marriage
   • Mistaken Identity
   • Victorian Conventions and Moral Restraints
   • Memory and Writing

   Then, have each group decorate a quarter of the bulletin board with photographs, drawings, printed images, or quotations relating to that motif.

5. Create a working time line of events in the play, beginning with Miss Prism's leaving the infant in her hand-bag and ending with the discovery that Jack's name is really Ernest.

6. Use the bulletin board to display some epigrams in *The Importance of Being Earnest*. A few can be found in the Quotations section of this LitPlan.

7. Fill the bulletin board with student-drawn images of characters or scenes in the play.

8. If you would rather have your students read the play aloud during class rather than individually and at home, you could decorate the bulletin board so that it looks like a playbill. You could list the characters' names down one side, and each day, write the name of the person reading that part. Character drawings or images are optional.

9. Post-literary criticism of *The Importance of Being Earnest*, theater reviews, or any upcoming performances of the play in your area on the bulletin board.

10. Make a bulletin board listing some or all of the vocabulary words for this unit. As you complete sections of the novel and discuss the vocabulary for each section, write the definitions on the bulletin board. If your board is one students face often, it will help them learn the words.

RELATED TOPICS - *The Importance of Being Earnest*

1. Victorian Era
2. Aesthetic Movement
3. Fin de siecle
4. The Dandy
5. Late 19th-Century Fashion
6. Governesses and Wards
7. The Town v. The Country

MORE ACTIVITIES - *The Importance of Being Earnest*

1. Have students create a social networking page for one of the characters in the play. They should make inferences about the character and include the following information:

   - a creative title for the page
   - a drawing or pasted image of the character
   - name
   - age
   - occupation
   - interests/hobbies
   - favorite book(s)
   - favorite movie(s)
   - favorite television show(s)
   - favorite quote(s)

   A worksheet is included for students to complete.

2. Using the Internet or library resources, look up the following allusions in *The Importance of Being Earnest*:

   Richard Wagner

   "Only relatives, or creditors, ever ring in that Wagnerian manner." (Act I)

   The French Revolution

   "To be born, or at any rate bred, in a hand-bag, whether it had handles or not, seems to me to display a contempt for the ordinary decencies of family life that reminds one of the worst excesses of the French Revolution." (Act I)

   Gorgon

   "Her mother is perfectly unbearable. Never met such a Gorgon...I don't really know what a Gorgon is like, but I am quite sure that Lady Bracknell is one." (Act I)

   Egeria

   "But I must not disturb Egeria and her pupil any longer." (Act II)

   Students should:

   - read about the allusion, and write a short two-three sentence definition or explanation of the person, event, or thing.

   - explain the meaning of the sentence in which the allusion is used.

   - determine why Oscar Wilde might have chosen to use that allusion; in other words, what does that allusion lend to the text?

3. Have students write twitter summaries for each of the three acts. The summaries should not exceed 140 characters. Allow students to use informal "text-speak" and incomplete sentences for this assignment.

4. Have students write a letter from one character to another, expressing his or her thoughts and feelings about what occurred in a particular scene.

    If students have difficulty choosing characters and a scene to write about, you could suggest the following:

    - Jack to Algernon about the cigarette case interrogation

    - Gwendolen to Jack about Lady Bracknell's disapproval of their engagement

    - Cecily to Algernon/"Ernest" about the imagined love affair between them that she wrote about in her diary
    - Gwendolen to Cecily about their misunderstanding and argument over tea

    - Lady Bracknell to Jack about the revelation of his true name and parents

5. Have students design an alternate cover to *The Importance of Being Earnest* by including all of the following:

    - the title and byline (*The Importance of Being Earnest* by Oscar Wilde)
    - an illustration of a character, group of characters, scene in the novel, or creative
    - representation of a theme or motif
    - a brief summary of the play that does not reveal the ending

6. Have your students write a short essay in which they critique the play. They should answer all of the following questions:

    Characters

    - Were the characters easy to relate to?
    - Were the characters complex, or were they superficial and predictable?
    - Did the characters remain consistent throughout the play?

    Plot

    - Did you find the play interesting? If so, was the play written in a way that maintained your interest? Did you find some parts of the play boring and dull?

    - Did you think the plot was believable? Was it properly resolved, or were there still some unanswered questions?

    Themes and Motifs

    - Did the play contain any themes or motifs?
    - If so, where the themes and motifs clearly presented and developed?

Style

- Was the characters' dialogue realistic? Why or why not?
- Did the playwright incorporate any literary devices in his writing?
- Overall, how sophisticated do you think the playwright's writing technique is?

Relevance to the 21st Century

- Even though this play was written at the end of the 19th century, more than a century ago, do you think it is still relevant in today's society? Why or why not?

Suitability for High School Students

- Do you think this play is appropriate for high school students?
- Is there anything a high school student could learn from this play? If so, what? If not, why not?

7. Have students imagine that they are casting a new film version of *The Importance of Being Earnest*. Who would they consider to play each role?

   Have them complete the following steps for each character:

   - Write a brief description of the character's physical appearance and attributes. Most of this information will need to be inferred, but other information, such as the characters' relative ages, can be found in the text.

   - Write a brief description of the character's personality. For instance, is the character kind or cruel? Tense or relaxed? Talkative or quiet?

   - Write the name of the actor or actress chosen to play that character and why he or she could play that character well.

8. Have your students stage, or simply write, an imaginary talk show interviewing the characters of *The Importance of Being Earnest*.

   Students should complete the following steps:

   - Write an introduction to be presented by the host, briefly explaining what happened to the characters in the play.

   - Choose four characters from the play, and write five questions that the host could ask each character. The questions should be probing and important enough to help the audience members gain a better understanding of what happened and how the characters feel about the events that occurred.

   - Answer the questions the way the characters likely would. In the responses, students should attempt to emulate how the character speaks.

   - Write a closing statement made by the talk show host.

- Students could complete this activity individually or in small groups. Additionally, students could act out their talk shows in front of the class or use video equipment, if it is available, to record the talk show in their free time.

9. Have students write a sequel to *The Importance of Being Earnest*, writing about what happens to the characters following the close of the play.

    If students need a little extra help, you could have them consider the following questions:

    - Do you think Jack and Gwendolen get married and live happily? Algernon and Cecily?

    - Would Jack, now Ernest, continue trying to find out more about his past? Would he have an identity crisis?

    - What might happen to Lady Bracknell? Would she continue to approve of the engagements? Would she change her mind and withdraw her consent?

    - What happens to Miss Prism? Does she fall in love with Dr. Chasuble? Is she held responsible for the incident with the baby in the hand-bag?

    - The sequels could either be written in prose or in the form of a play.

10. Hold a class debate on one of the following issues:

    - to what extent families should be involved in engagements and marriages
    - whether it is ever morally correct to deceive another person
    - the reliability of history, taking into account how diaries and letter are treated in this play
    - if the events in the play could occur in real life

SOCIAL NETWORKING PAGE - *The Importance of Being Earnest*

_____
[Put the title of the character's page on the line above.]

[Draw or paste a picture of the character.]

Name: _____

Age: _____

Occupation: _____

Interests/Hobbies: _____
_____
_____
_____

Favorite Book(s): _____
_____
_____
_____

Favorite Movie(s): _____
_____
_____
_____

Favorite Television Show(s): _____
_____
_____
_____

Favorite Quote(s): _____
_____
_____
_____

EXTRA DISCUSSION QUESTIONS/WRITING ASSIGNMENTS - *The Importance of Being Earnest*

Interpretive:

1. At the beginning of the play, Algernon says to Lane, "I don't play accurately...any one can play accurately...but I play with wonderful expression. As far as the piano is concerned, sentiment is my forte. I keep science for Life." What can you infer about Algernon's character by this statement, and how do the values and beliefs expressed explain his behavior in the play?

2. What can be inferred about Cecily's character by her watering the plants at the beginning of the scene, her reasons for disliking German, her opinions on writing, and her fears about meeting Ernest? Develop your character study into a short essay.

3. Explain the power struggle between Cecily and Gwendolen in Act II, when they meet for the first time. How does each woman attempt to demean the other and make herself look better?

4. Are the female characters in this play (e.g., Cecily, Gwendolen, Lady Bracknell, and Miss Prism) presented as stereotypes, intentional deviations from stereotypes, or mentally and emotionally complex individuals? Use textual examples to support your answer.

Critical:

5. Compare and contrast Algernon's Bunburying and Jack's visiting his fictitious brother Ernest. Why does each character deceive his friends and family members, and how do the differences in their reasons establish the characters as foils?

6. In Act I, several ideas about love are expressed. Identify these ideas, and explain how a conflict between them underlies the plot of the play.

7. Lady Bracknell is reluctant to allow Gwendolen to marry Jack because his parentage is uncertain: he was found in a hand-bag in Victoria Station, and there is no way to determine his social standing. In general, how is the issue of class status treated in this play? Explain your answer with examples from the text.

8. What is the view of Jack presented by Cecily? Does this validate or refute the statements he makes in Act I about his life in the country and how he presents himself to his ward?

9. In the scene where Jack arrives at the country house, ignorant of the fact that Algernon is there, how does Oscar Wilde use dramatic irony to create suspense? Additionally, does the suspense merely raise the audience's interest, or does it place emphasis on a certain scene, theme, or motif? Explain your answer.

10. In Act II, what does writing...in the form of diary entries, letters, and manuscripts...suggest about the importance of the written word and the nature of history?

11. In Act III, what does the exchange between Lady Bracknell and Jack, in which they discuss Cecily's background, suggest about marriage and match-making in the Victorian Era?

12. What seems to be the purpose of eating in this play (e.g., the cucumber sandwiches and the muffins)? Does the act of eating contribute to a theme or motif in the play? Does it indicate the emotional states of the characters? Justify your response with examples from the text.

13. One of the literary techniques that is frequently utilized by Oscar Wilde is punning. In a well-organized essay, identify uses of puns in the play, and explain why they are used. Be sure to take character development, the ridicule and subversion of Victorian conventions, and the expression of uncommon views into consideration.

14. In a well-organized essay, trace the theme of the creation, discovery, and evaluation of identity in this play.

Critical/Personal Response:

15. Before the cigarette case interrogation scene, Algernon seems to know that the case belongs to Jack. If Algernon had merely given Jack the case without asking questions, how would this play have been different?

16. When Jack's friends learn of Ernest's death and then discover that Ernest is alive and in the dining-room, they do not seem bothered. Dr. Chasuble expresses his joy, and Miss Prism remarks that Ernest's "sudden return seems...particularly distressing." Once Cecily and Algernon enter the room, the characters forget that Ernest was "dead." Do you think this scene is realistic? How would you react if you were informed someone you barely knew had died, but was alive in your home? Develop your ideas into a short essay.

17. Do you feel satisfied with the ending of the play? Are the revelation and the new character relationships it creates realistic? Is the ending foreshadowed, or does it seem unexpected? Is it realistic or contrived? Develop your ideas into a well-organized essay.

QUOTATION WORKSHEET - *The Importance of Being Earnest*

1. When one is in town one amuses oneself. When one is in the country one amuses other people.

2. I really don't see anything romantic in proposing. It is very romantic to be in love. But there is nothing romantic about a definite proposal. Why, one may be accepted. One usually is, I believe. Then the excitement is all over. The very essence of romance is uncertainty. If ever I get married, I'll certainly try to forget the fact.

3. Well, in the first place girls never marry the men they flirt with. Girl's don't think it right....It is a great truth. It accounts for the extraordinary number of bachelors that one sees all over the place.

4. Oh! it is absurd to have a hard-and-fast rule about what one should read and what one shouldn't. More than half of modern culture depends on what one shouldn't read.

5. You have always told me [your name] was Ernest. I have introduced you to everyone as Ernest. You answer to the name of Ernest. You look as if your name was Ernest. You are the most earnest-looking person I ever saw in my life. It is perfectly absurd your saying that your name isn't Ernest. It's on your cards.

6. We live, as I hope you know...in an age of ideals. The fact is constantly mentioned in the more expensive monthly magazines, and has reached the provincial pulpits, I am told: and my ideal has always been to love some one of the name of Ernest. There is something in that name that inspires absolute confidence.

7. An engagement should come on a young girl as a surprise, pleasant or unpleasant, as the case may be. It is hardly a matter that she could be allowed to arrange for herself.

8. Ignorance is like a delicate exotic fruit; touch it and the bloom is gone. The whole theory of modern education is radically unsound. Fortunately in England, at any rate, education produces no effect whatsoever. If it did, it would prove a serious danger to the upper classes, and probably lead to acts of violence in Grosvenor Square.

9. I am sick to death of cleverness. Everybody is clever now-a-days. You can't go anywhere without meeting clever people. The thing has become an absolute public nuisance. I wish to goodness we had a few fools left.

10. Ernest, we may never be married. From the expression on mamma's face I fear we never shall. Few parents now-a-days pay any regard to what their children say to them. The old-fashioned respect for the young is fast dying out. Whatever influence I ever had over mamma, I lost at the age of three. But although she may prevent us from becoming man and wife, and I may marry someone else, and marry often, nothing that she can possibly do can alter my eternal devotion to you.

11. I am not in favour of this modern mania for turning bad people into good people at a moment's notice. As a man sows so let him reap.

12. I keep a diary in order to enter the wonderful secrets of my life. If I didn't write them down, I should probably forget all about them...[Memory] usually chronicles the things that have never happened, and couldn't possibly have happened. I believe that Memory is responsible for nearly all the three-volume novels that Mudie sends us.

13. The good ended happily, and the bad unhappily. That is what Fiction means.

14. And you do not seem to realise, dear Doctor, that by persistently remaining single, a man converts himself into a permanent public temptation. Men should be more careful; this very celibacy leads weaker vessels astray....No married man is ever attractive except to his wife.

15. You must not laugh at me, darling, but it had always been a girlish dream of mine to love some one whose name was Ernest. There is something in that name that seems to inspire absolute confidence. I pity any poor married woman whose husband is not called Ernest.

16. What an impetuous boy he is! I like his hair so much. I must enter his proposal in my diary.

17. Outside the family circle, papa, I am glad to say, is entirely unknown. I think that is quite as it should be. The home seems to me to be the proper sphere for the man. And certainly once a man begins to neglect his domestic duties he becomes painfully effeminate, does he not?

18. Ernest has a strong upright nature. He is the very soul of truth and honour. Disloyalty would be as impossible to him as deception. But even men of the noblest possible moral character are extremely susceptible to the influence of the physical charms of others. Modern, no less than Ancient History, supplies us with many most painful examples of what I refer to. If it were not so, indeed, History would be unreadable.

19. I never travel without my diary. On should always have something sensational to read in the train.

20. I do not know whether there is anything peculiarly exciting in the air of this particular part of Hertfordshire, but the number of engagements that go on seems to me considerably above the proper average that statistics have laid down for our guidance.

21. To speak frankly, I am not in favour of long engagements. They give people the opportunity of finding out each other's character before marriage, which I think is never advisable.

UNIT WORD LIST - *The Importance of Being Earnest*

No.	Word	Clue/Definition
1.	ALGERNON	Gwendolen's cousin
2.	AUGUSTA	Lady Bracknell's first name
3.	BRACKNELL	Gwendolen's father: Lord _____
4.	BRIGHTON	The line of the station where the baby was found
5.	BUNBURY	Algernon's fictitious friend
6.	CARDEW	Cecily's last name
7.	CECILY	The name of Jack's ward
8.	CHASUBLE	The name of the rector: Dr. _____
9.	CUCUMBER	The sandwiches Algernon made for his aunt's visit
10.	DIARY	Where Cecily and Gwendolen record their thoughts
11.	EMPIRE	The club to which Algernon and Jack belong
12.	ERNEST	The name of Jack's fictitious brother
13.	FAIRFAX	Gwendolen's last name
14.	GENERAL	Jack's father's title in the army
15.	GWENDOLEN	Jack's fiancée
16.	HALFMOON	The street on which Algernon lives
17.	HANDBAG	The baby was discovered in a _____
18.	JACK	The boy Mr. Thomas Cardew adopted
19.	MANUSCRIPT	What Miss Prism accidentally swapped with the baby
20.	MONCRIEFF	Algernon's last name
21.	MUFFINS	The baked good that Algernon enjoys eating
22.	PARIS	The city in which Ernest dies from a severe chill
23.	PIANO	The instrument Algernon plays
24.	PRISM	Cecily's governess: Miss _____
25.	THREE	The number of months Cecily has been engaged to Ernest
26.	VICTORIA	The train station where the baby was found
27.	WOOLTON	The location of Jack's country house
28.	WORTHING	The Sussex resort to which Mr. Thomas Cardew was traveling

WORD SEARCH - *The Importance of Being Earnest*

```
B  A  L  G  E  R  N  O  N  W  K  C  B  D  H
R  R  F  A  I  R  F  A  X  O  Q  H  U  S  A
A  Z  I  B  C  V  B  G  Q  O  V  A  N  R  N
C  N  T  G  F  M  N  Z  P  L  I  S  B  V  D
K  F  P  Y  H  I  O  D  C  T  C  U  U  C  B
N  E  E  R  H  T  Q  N  Y  O  T  B  R  A  A
E  R  T  T  C  N  O  Q  C  N  O  L  Y  R  G
L  Y  R  H  D  T  F  N  D  R  R  E  Q  D  W
L  O  C  E  C  I  L  Y  M  I  I  L  M  E  E
W  L  P  P  A  U  G  U  S  T  A  E  P  W  N
J  S  I  R  A  P  F  X  J  R  R  R  F  W  D
V  J  A  P  V  F  B  L  E  I  I  N  Y  F  O
Z  A  N  M  I  W  F  N  P  S  P  E  R  K  L
F  C  O  N  P  M  E  M  M  L  J  S  H  S  E
P  K  S  P  L  G  E  K  S  G  D  T  N  B  N
```

ALGERNON	EMPIRE	PARIS
AUGUSTA	ERNEST	PIANO
BRACKNELL	FAIRFAX	PRISM
BRIGHTON	GENERAL	THREE
BUNBURY	GWENDOLEN	VICTORIA
CARDEW	HANDBAG	WOOLTON
CECILY	JACK	WORTHING
CHASUBLE	MONCRIEFF	
DIARY	MUFFINS	

WORD SEARCH ANSWER KEY - *The Importance of Being Earnest*

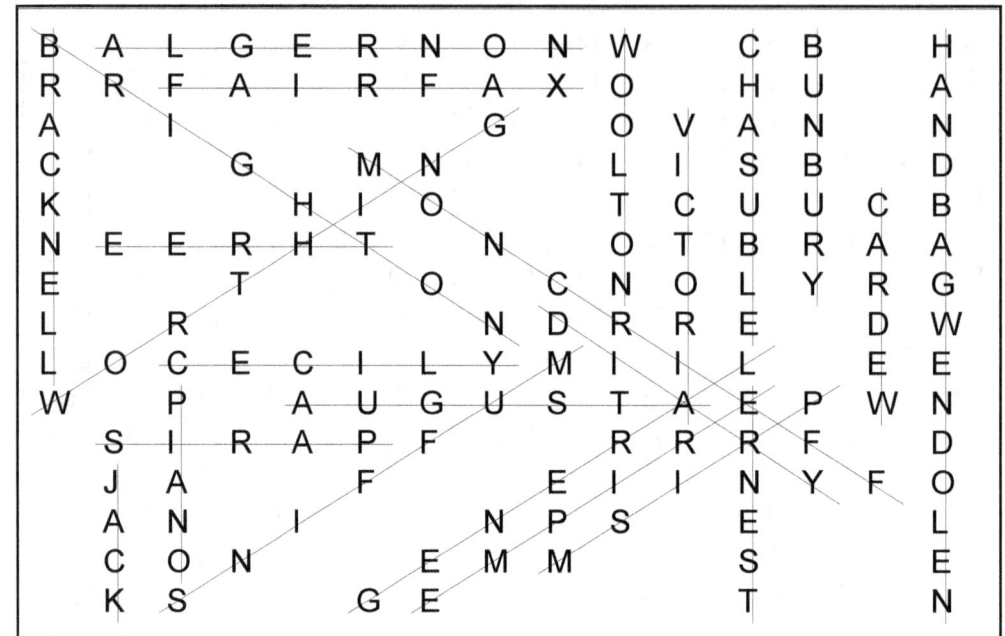

ALGERNON	EMPIRE	PARIS
AUGUSTA	ERNEST	PIANO
BRACKNELL	FAIRFAX	PRISM
BRIGHTON	GENERAL	THREE
BUNBURY	GWENDOLEN	VICTORIA
CARDEW	HANDBAG	WOOLTON
CECILY	JACK	WORTHING
CHASUBLE	MONCRIEFF	
DIARY	MUFFINS	

CROSSWORD PUZZLE - *The Importance of Being Earnest*

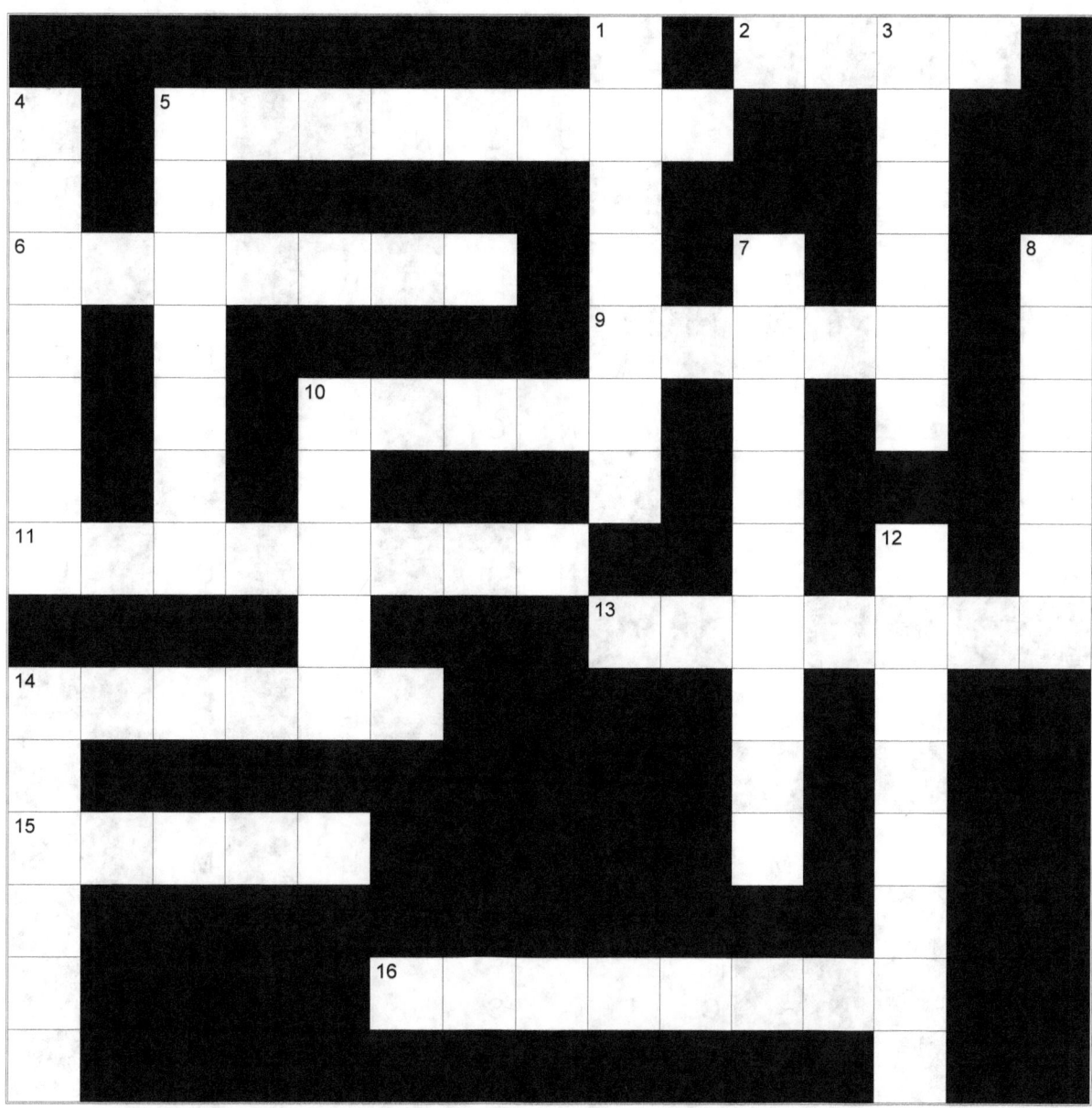

Across

2. The boy Mr. Thomas Cardew adopted
5. The street on which Algernon lives
6. Jack's father's title in the army
9. The number of months Cecily has been engaged to Ernest
10. The instrument Algernon plays
11. Gwendolen's cousin
13. Algernon's fictitious friend
14. The name of Jack's fictitious brother
15. Cecily's governess: Miss _____
16. The name of the rector: Dr. _____

Down

1. The location of Jack's country house
3. Cecily's last name
4. Lady Bracknell's first name
5. The baby was discovered in a _____
7. Gwendolen's father: Lord _____
8. The name of Jack's ward
10. The city in which Ernest dies from a severe chill
12. The sandwiches Algernon made for his aunt's visit
14. The club to which Algernon and Jack belong

CROSSWORD PUZZLE ANSWER KEY - *The Importance of Being Earnest*

								¹W		²J	A	³C	K	
⁴A		⁵H	A	L	F	M	O	O	N			A		
U		A						O				R		
⁶G	E	N	E	R	A	L		L		⁷B		D		⁸C
U		D					⁹T	H	R	E	E			E
S		B		¹⁰P	I	A	N	O		A		W		C
T		A		A			N			C				I
¹¹A	L	G	E	R	N	O	N			K		¹²C		L
				I				¹³B	U	N	B	U	R	Y
¹⁴E	R	N	E	S	T			E		E		C		
M								L				U		
¹⁵P	R	I	S	M				L				M		
I												B		
R				¹⁶C	H	A	S	U	B	L	E			
E											R			

Across

2. The boy Mr. Thomas Cardew adopted
5. The street on which Algernon lives
6. Jack's father's title in the army
9. The number of months Cecily has been engaged to Ernest
10. The instrument Algernon plays
11. Gwendolen's cousin
13. Algernon's fictitious friend
14. The name of Jack's fictitious brother
15. Cecily's governess: Miss _____
16. The name of the rector: Dr. _____

Down

1. The location of Jack's country house
3. Cecily's last name
4. Lady Bracknell's first name
5. The baby was discovered in a _____
7. Gwendolen's father: Lord _____
8. The name of Jack's ward
10. The city in which Ernest dies from a severe chill
12. The sandwiches Algernon made for his aunt's visit
14. The club to which Algernon and Jack belong

MATCHING 1 - *The Importance of Being Earnest*

___ 1. BRIGHTON   A. Gwendolen's last name

___ 2. ERNEST   B. The Sussex resort to which Mr. Thomas Cardew was traveling

___ 3. JACK   C. The line of the station where the baby was found

___ 4. ALGERNON   D. The name of the rector: Dr. _____

___ 5. PRISM   E. Jack's fiancée

___ 6. CHASUBLE   F. Lady Bracknell's first name

___ 7. GWENDOLEN   G. Cecily's governess: Miss _____

___ 8. FAIRFAX   H. The boy Mr. Thomas Cardew adopted

___ 9. AUGUSTA   I. Gwendolen's father: Lord _____

___ 10. BRACKNELL   J. Cecily's last name

___ 11. MONCRIEFF   K. Gwendolen's cousin

___ 12. WORTHING   L. The name of Jack's ward

___ 13. CARDEW   M. The name of Jack's fictitious brother

___ 14. VICTORIA   N. The train station where the baby was found

___ 15. CECILY   O. Algernon's last name

MATCHING 1 ANSWER KEY - *The Importance of Being Earnest*

C	1. BRIGHTON	A.	Gwendolen's last name
M	2. ERNEST	B.	The Sussex resort to which Mr. Thomas Cardew was traveling
H	3. JACK	C.	The line of the station where the baby was found
K	4. ALGERNON	D.	The name of the rector: Dr. _____
G	5. PRISM	E.	Jack's fiancée
D	6. CHASUBLE	F.	Lady Bracknell's first name
E	7. GWENDOLEN	G.	Cecily's governess: Miss _____
A	8. FAIRFAX	H.	The boy Mr. Thomas Cardew adopted
F	9. AUGUSTA	I.	Gwendolen's father: Lord _____
I	10. BRACKNELL	J.	Cecily's last name
O	11. MONCRIEFF	K.	Gwendolen's cousin
B	12. WORTHING	L.	The name of Jack's ward
J	13. CARDEW	M.	The name of Jack's fictitious brother
N	14. VICTORIA	N.	The train station where the baby was found
L	15. CECILY	O.	Algernon's last name

MATCHING 2 - *The Importance of Being Earnest*

____ 1.   CUCUMBER   A.   The instrument Algernon plays

____ 2.   GENERAL   B.   Algernon's fictitious friend

____ 3.   PARIS   C.   The street on which Algernon lives

____ 4.   EMPIRE   D.   The club to which Algernon and Jack belong

____ 5.   DIARY   E.   What Miss Prism accidentally swapped with the baby

____ 6.   THREE   F.   The line of the station where the baby was found

____ 7.   BUNBURY   G.   The baby was discovered in a _____

____ 8.   PIANO   H.   The city in which Ernest dies from a severe chill

____ 9.   HALFMOON   I.   Where Cecily and Gwendolen record their thoughts

____ 10. HANDBAG   J.   The sandwiches Algernon made for his aunt's visit

____ 11. BRIGHTON   K.   The number of months Cecily has been engaged to Ernest

____ 12. VICTORIA   L.   The baked good that Algernon enjoys eating

____ 13. WOOLTON   M.   Jack's father's title in the army

____ 14. MUFFINS   N.   The train station where the baby was found

____ 15. MANUSCRIPT   O.   The location of Jack's country house

MATCHING 2 ANSWER KEY - *The Importance of Being Earnest*

J	1. CUCUMBER		A.	The instrument Algernon plays
M	2. GENERAL		B.	Algernon's fictitious friend
H	3. PARIS		C.	The street on which Algernon lives
D	4. EMPIRE		D.	The club to which Algernon and Jack belong
I	5. DIARY		E.	What Miss Prism accidentally swapped with the baby
K	6. THREE		F.	The line of the station where the baby was found
B	7. BUNBURY		G.	The baby was discovered in a _____
A	8. PIANO		H.	The city in which Ernest dies from a severe chill
C	9. HALFMOON		I.	Where Cecily and Gwendolen record their thoughts
G	10. HANDBAG		J.	The sandwiches Algernon made for his aunt's visit
F	11. BRIGHTON		K.	The number of months Cecily has been engaged to Ernest
N	12. VICTORIA		L.	The baked good that Algernon enjoys eating
O	13. WOOLTON		M.	Jack's father's title in the army
L	14. MUFFINS		N.	The train station where the baby was found
E	15. MANUSCRIPT		O.	The location of Jack's country house

JUGGLE LETTERS 1 - *The Importance of Being Earnest*

_____	= 1. LOOOWTN
	The location of Jack's country house
_____	= 2. NBYRUBU
	Algernon's fictitious friend
_____	= 3. HOMLONFA
	The street on which Algernon lives
_____	= 4. GTRHONBI
	The line of the station where the baby was found
_____	= 5. AIIVOCRT
	The train station where the baby was found
_____	= 6. LCIYCE
	The name of Jack's ward
_____	= 7. RSTEEN
	The name of Jack's fictitious brother
_____	= 8. NLREAONG
	Gwendolen's cousin
_____	= 9. SCULHBEA
	The name of the rector: Dr. _____
_____	= 10. NDELENOWG
	Jack's fiancée
_____	= 11. RLNKALEBC
	Gwendolen's father: Lord _____
_____	= 12. FIFOCMNRE
	Algernon's last name
_____	= 13. THRNWOGI
	The Sussex resort to which Mr. Thomas Cardew was traveling
_____	= 14. FSIUMNF
	The baked good that Algernon enjoys eating
_____	= 15. NRUAPSTCIM
	What Miss Prism accidentally swapped with the baby

JUGGLE LETTERS 1 ANSWER KEY - *The Importance of Being Earnest*

WOOLTON	= 1.	LOOOWTN
		The location of Jack's country house
BUNBURY	= 2.	NBYRUBU
		Algernon's fictitious friend
HALFMOON	= 3.	HOMLONFA
		The street on which Algernon lives
BRIGHTON	= 4.	GTRHONBI
		The line of the station where the baby was found
VICTORIA	= 5.	AIIVOCRT
		The train station where the baby was found
CECILY	= 6.	LCIYCE
		The name of Jack's ward
ERNEST	= 7.	RSTEEN
		The name of Jack's fictitious brother
ALGERNON	= 8.	NLREAONG
		Gwendolen's cousin
CHASUBLE	= 9.	SCULHBEA
		The name of the rector: Dr. _____
GWENDOLEN	= 10.	NDELENOWG
		Jack's fiancée
BRACKNELL	= 11.	RLNKALEBC
		Gwendolen's father: Lord _____
MONCRIEFF	= 12.	FIFOCMNRE
		Algernon's last name
WORTHING	= 13.	THRNWOGI
		The Sussex resort to which Mr. Thomas Cardew was traveling
MUFFINS	= 14.	FSIUMNF
		The baked good that Algernon enjoys eating
MANUSCRIPT	= 15.	NRUAPSTCIM
		What Miss Prism accidentally swapped with the baby

JUGGLE LETTERS 2 - *The Importance of Being Earnest*

_____ = 1. NBADGHA
   The baby was discovered in a _____

_____ = 2. EEGRANL
   Jack's father's title in the army

_____ = 3. PIEEMR
   The club to which Algernon and Jack belong

_____ = 4. BURNBUY
   Algernon's fictitious friend

_____ = 5. OOFNHLMA
   The street on which Algernon lives

_____ = 6. TESERN
   The name of Jack's fictitious brother

_____ = 7. GOLNRANE
   Gwendolen's cousin

_____ = 8. EWODLNNEG
   Jack's fiancée

_____ = 9. FOIMENCFR
   Algernon's last name

_____ = 10. OHTNWGRI
   The Sussex resort to which Mr. Thomas Cardew was traveling

_____ = 11. MCEUURCB
   The sandwiches Algernon made for his aunt's visit

_____ = 12. OOTWNOL
   The location of Jack's country house

_____ = 13. IRTOCIVA
   The train station where the baby was found

_____ = 14. ROTGINBH
   The line of the station where the baby was found

_____ = 15. TPSMURANCI
   What Miss Prism accidentally swapped with the baby

JUGGLE LETTERS 2 ANSWER KEY - *The Importance of Being Earnest*

HANDBAG	= 1.	NBADGHA	
		The baby was discovered in a _____	
GENERAL	= 2.	EEGRANL	
		Jack's father's title in the army	
EMPIRE	= 3.	PIEEMR	
		The club to which Algernon and Jack belong	
BUNBURY	= 4.	BURNBUY	
		Algernon's fictitious friend	
HALFMOON	= 5.	OOFNHLMA	
		The street on which Algernon lives	
ERNEST	= 6.	TESERN	
		The name of Jack's fictitious brother	
ALGERNON	= 7.	GOLNRANE	
		Gwendolen's cousin	
GWENDOLEN	= 8.	EWODLNNEG	
		Jack's fiancée	
MONCRIEFF	= 9.	FOIMENCFR	
		Algernon's last name	
WORTHING	= 10.	OHTNWGRI	
		The Sussex resort to which Mr. Thomas Cardew was traveling	
CUCUMBER	= 11.	MCEUURCB	
		The sandwiches Algernon made for his aunt's visit	
WOOLTON	= 12.	OOTWNOL	
		The location of Jack's country house	
VICTORIA	= 13.	IRTOCIVA	
		The train station where the baby was found	
BRIGHTON	= 14.	ROTGINBH	
		The line of the station where the baby was found	
MANUSCRIPT	= 15.	TPSMURANCI	
		What Miss Prism accidentally swapped with the baby	

VOCABULARY RESOURCE MATERIALS

VOCABULARY WORD LIST - *The Importance of Being Earnest*

No.	Word	Clue/Definition
1.	ADMISSION	a confession or an acknowledgment
2.	APPRISED	informed; given knowledge of
3.	BECOMING	attractive or flattering
4.	CANDIDLY	truthfully and sincerely
5.	CAPACIOUS	spacious or having the ability to hold a lot
6.	COMMENDED	praised or complimented
7.	COMMERCE	relating to trade or business
8.	CONSTITUTED	composed or constructed of
9.	CONSTITUTION	a person's physical and mental well being
10.	CREDULITY	believability; inspiring trust and faith in an idea
11.	CYNICAL	bitter and distrustful
12.	DEMONSTRATIVE	expressive or affectionate
13.	DEMORALIZING	depressing; disheartening
14.	DIGNIFIED	honorable and distinguished
15.	DISPOSITION	a person's behavior and attitude
16.	DOMESTICITY	relating to the home or the household; in this usage, a nickname
17.	DOTING	overly fond of and permissive
18.	EFFRONTERY	rudeness or shamelessness
19.	EMIGRATING	leaving one's country to live in another
20.	ENGAGED	busy or occupied; having plans with someone or to do something
21.	EPIDEMIC	a widespread disease or illness
22.	EQUANIMITY	calmness and composure
23.	EXPURGATIONS	items that are removed from a collection
24.	FORTE	a strength or specialty
25.	GLIBLY	spoken flippantly or without prior thought
26.	GOVERNESS	a female who lives with and teaches children in a private home
27.	GRAVITY	seriousness; coldness
28.	GROTESQUE	unnatural, bizarre, and hideous
29.	HEREDITARY	can be passed from an individual to his or her offspring
30.	IMPETUOUS	rash and careless
31.	INDECOROUS	improper; unmannerly
32.	INDIGNANT	disgusted or annoyed
33.	INQUIRIES	investigations; acts of questioning or obtaining information
34.	INSUPERABLE	unable to be bypassed or overlooked
35.	INVALID	a person who is in frequently in poor health
36.	IRRETRIEVABLY	unable to be repaired or recovered
37.	LAVISHED	given in abundance

No.	Word	Clue/Definition
38.	LAX	loose or careless; not strict
39.	MACHINATIONS	schemes or tricks
40.	MELANCHOLY	depressing or spiritless
41.	MELODRAMATIC	overemotional and theatrical
42.	MERCENARY	providing a service only for financial gain
43.	METAPHYSICAL	abstract and philosophical
44.	MISANTHROPE	an individual who hates people
45.	NEOLOGISTIC	relating to a word that has just been created
46.	NOTORIOUS	well-known for terrible reasons
47.	OSTENTATIOUSLY	in a showy manner; extravagantly
48.	PERAMBULATOR	a baby carriage
49.	PHILANTHROPIC	having to do with the giving of money or services to help others
50.	PRELIMINARY	done beforehand or in preparation for
51.	PRETENSE	a deception or false claim
52.	PROPOUNDING	putting forth for others to consider
53.	QUAIL	to cringe with fear
54.	QUIXOTIC	dreamy, romantic, and idealistic
55.	RADICALLY	completely and thoroughly
56.	REPENTANCE	an expression of regret for doing something wrong
57.	SEMI-RECUMBENT	half-reclined; almost lying down
58.	SENTENTIOUSLY	self-righteously; expressing wise sayings and aphorisms
59.	SENTIMENT	an emotion or feeling
60.	SOLICITORS	lawyers or legal advisers
61.	SOLITUDE	the state of being alone; seclusion
62.	TEMPERANCE	sobriety; abstaining from drinking alcohol
63.	TERMINUS	a train or bus station
64.	TRIVIALITY	something unimportant and superficial
65.	TUTELAGE	protection or care by a guardian or tutor
66.	UNSOUND	impaired; not well-formed
67.	UTILITARIAN	relating to usefulness instead of grace, beauty, or sophistication
68.	VACILLATING	indecisive or wavering

VOCABULARY WORD SEARCH - *The Importance of Being Earnest*

```
C C I M E D I P E E Q S E D N
R O L C Y N I C A L U O X E O
E M L P S F Z W T B I L P M T
D M W N E G N Q R A X I U O O
U E J K N N G E I R O T R N R
L R D O T I N G V E T U G S I
I C S X E P I A I P I D A T O
T E U R N R D L A U C E T R U
Y F O R T E N E L S L Y I A S
M C I L I T U T I N A R O T G
H B C Y O E O U T I X T N I L
M V A N U N P T Y B B M S V I
R G P V S S O D E G A G N E B
Q U A I L E R D E H S I V A L
L N C B Y K P C A N D I D L Y
```

CANDIDLY	EPIDEMIC	PRETENSE
CAPACIOUS	EXPURGATIONS	PROPOUNDING
COMMERCE	FORTE	QUAIL
CREDULITY	GLIBLY	QUIXOTIC
CYNICAL	INSUPERABLE	SENTENTIOUSLY
DEMONSTRATIVE	LAVISHED	SOLITUDE
DOTING	LAX	TRIVIALITY
ENGAGED	NOTORIOUS	TUTELAGE

VOCABULARY WORD SEARCH ANSWER KEY - *The Importance of Being Earnest*

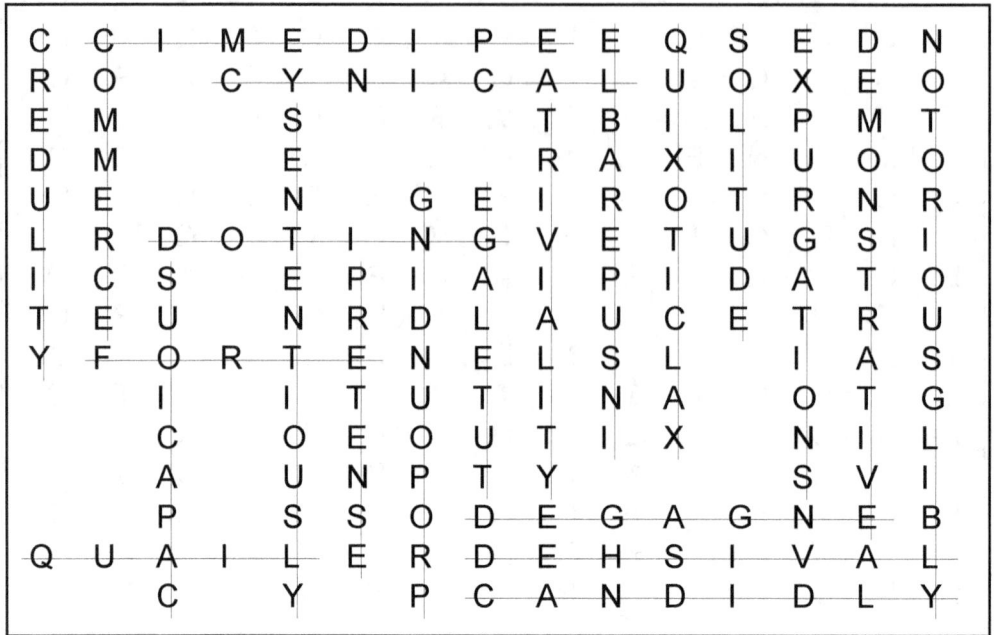

CANDIDLY	EPIDEMIC	PRETENSE
CAPACIOUS	EXPURGATIONS	PROPOUNDING
COMMERCE	FORTE	QUAIL
CREDULITY	GLIBLY	QUIXOTIC
CYNICAL	INSUPERABLE	SENTENTIOUSLY
DEMONSTRATIVE	LAVISHED	SOLITUDE
DOTING	LAX	TRIVIALITY
ENGAGED	NOTORIOUS	TUTELAGE

VOCABULARY CROSSWORD PUZZLE - *The Importance of Being Earnest*

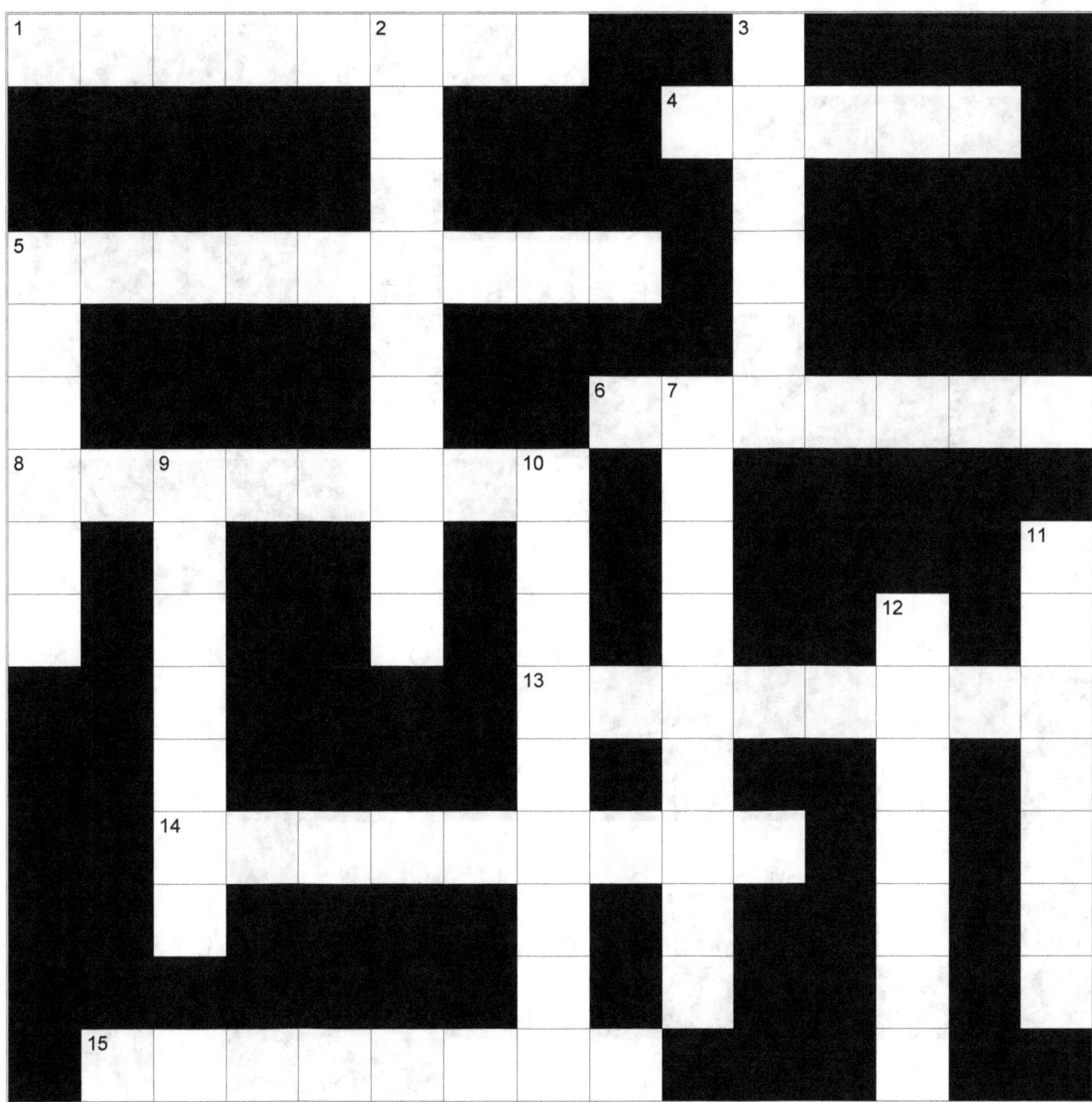

Across

1. truthfully and sincerely
4. a strength or specialty
5. a female who lives with and teaches children in a private home
6. busy or occupied; having plans with someone or to do something
8. attractive or flattering
13. a train or bus station
14. a confession or an acknowledgment
15. informed; given knowledge of

Down

2. honorable and distinguished
3. overly fond of and permissive
5. spoken flippantly or without prior thought
7. well-known for terrible reasons
9. bitter and distrustful
10. unnatural, bizarre, and hideous
11. impaired; not well-formed
12. a person who is in frequently in poor health

VOCABULARY CROSSWORD PUZZLE ANSWER KEY - *The Importance of Being Earnest*

Across

1. truthfully and sincerely
4. a strength or specialty
5. a female who lives with and teaches children in a private home
6. busy or occupied; having plans with someone or to do something
8. attractive or flattering
13. a train or bus station
14. a confession or an acknowledgment
15. informed; given knowledge of

Down

2. honorable and distinguished
3. overly fond of and permissive
5. spoken flippantly or without prior thought
7. well-known for terrible reasons
9. bitter and distrustful
10. unnatural, bizarre, and hideous
11. impaired; not well-formed
12. a person who is in frequently in poor health

VOCABULARY MATCHING 1 - *The Importance of Being Earnest*

____ 1. SENTENTIOUSLY   A. leaving one's country to live in another

____ 2. GLIBLY   B. well known for terrible reasons

____ 3. EQUANIMITY   C. truthfully and sincerely

____ 4. EMIGRATING   D. given in abundance

____ 5. DOMESTICITY   E. a confession or an acknowledgment

____ 6. DEMORALIZING   F. calmness and composure

____ 7. CREDULITY   G. unnatural, bizarre, and hideous

____ 8. COMMERCE   H. spoken flippantly or without prior thought

____ 9. CANDIDLY   I. relating to trade or business

____ 10. GROTESQUE   J. having to do with the giving of money or services to help others

____ 11. INDECOROUS   K. self-righteously; expressing wise sayings and aphorisms

____ 12. RADICALLY   L. abstract and philosophical

____ 13. PROPOUNDING   M. improper; unmannerly

____ 14. PHILANTHROPIC   N. depressing; disheartening

____ 15. NOTORIOUS   O. unable to be bypassed or overlooked

____ 16. METAPHYSICAL   P. believability; inspiring trust and faith in an idea

____ 17. MELANCHOLY   Q. depressing or spiritless

____ 18. LAVISHED   R. putting forth for others to consider

____ 19. INSUPERABLE   S. relating to the home or the household; in this usage, a nickname

____ 20. ADMISSION   T. completely and thoroughly

VOCABULARY MATCHING 1 ANSWER KEY - *The Importance of Being Earnest*

K	1.	SENTENTIOUSLY	A.	leaving one's country to live in another
H	2.	GLIBLY	B.	well known for terrible reasons
F	3.	EQUANIMITY	C.	truthfully and sincerely
A	4.	EMIGRATING	D.	given in abundance
S	5.	DOMESTICITY	E.	a confession or an acknowledgment
N	6.	DEMORALIZING	F.	calmness and composure
P	7.	CREDULITY	G.	unnatural, bizarre, and hideous
I	8.	COMMERCE	H.	spoken flippantly or without prior thought
C	9.	CANDIDLY	I.	relating to trade or business
G	10.	GROTESQUE	J.	having to do with the giving of money or services to help others
M	11.	INDECOROUS	K.	self-righteously; expressing wise sayings and aphorisms
T	12.	RADICALLY	L.	abstract and philosophical
R	13.	PROPOUNDING	M.	improper; unmannerly
J	14.	PHILANTHROPIC	N.	depressing; disheartening
B	15.	NOTORIOUS	O.	unable to be bypassed or overlooked
L	16.	METAPHYSICAL	P.	believability; inspiring trust and faith in an idea
Q	17.	MELANCHOLY	Q.	depressing or spiritless
D	18.	LAVISHED	R.	putting forth for others to consider
O	19.	INSUPERABLE	S.	relating to the home or the household; in this usage, a nickname
E	20.	ADMISSION	T.	completely and thoroughly

VOCABULARY MATCHING 2 - *The Importance of Being Earnest*

____ 1. APPRISED A. busy or occupied; having plans with someone or to do something

____ 2. INVALID B. honorable and distinguished

____ 3. LAX C. a female who lives with and teaches children in a private home

____ 4. MELODRAMATIC D. a person who is in frequently in poor health

____ 5. MISANTHROPE E. items that are removed from a collection

____ 6. PRELIMINARY F. can be passed from an individual to his or her offspring

____ 7. QUAIL G. informed; given knowledge of

____ 8. REPENTANCE H. overemotional and theatrical

____ 9. TEMPERANCE I. overly fond of and permissive

____ 10. INDIGNANT J. indecisive or wavering

____ 11. HEREDITARY K. spacious or having the ability to hold a lot

____ 12. CAPACIOUS L. disgusted or annoyed

____ 13. CONSTITUTED M. an individual who hates people

____ 14. CYNICAL N. done beforehand or in preparation for

____ 15. DIGNIFIED O. bitter and distrustful

____ 16. DOTING P. sobriety; abstaining from drinking alcohol

____ 17. ENGAGED Q. to cringe with fear

____ 18. EXPURGATIONS R. loose or careless; not strict

____ 19. GOVERNESS S. composed or constructed of

____ 20. VACILLATING T. an expression of regret for doing something wrong

VOCABULARY MATCHING 2 ANSWER KEY - *The Importance of Being Earnest*

G	1. APPRISED		A.	busy or occupied; having plans with someone or to do something
D	2. INVALID		B.	honorable and distinguished
R	3. LAX		C.	a female who lives with and teaches children in a private home
H	4. MELODRAMATIC		D.	a person who is in frequently in poor health
M	5. MISANTHROPE		E.	items that are removed from a collection
N	6. PRELIMINARY		F.	can be passed from an individual to his or her offspring
Q	7. QUAIL		G.	informed; given knowledge of
T	8. REPENTANCE		H.	overemotional and theatrical
P	9. TEMPERANCE		I.	overly fond of and permissive
L	10. INDIGNANT		J.	indecisive or wavering
F	11. HEREDITARY		K.	spacious or having the ability to hold a lot
K	12. CAPACIOUS		L.	disgusted or annoyed
S	13. CONSTITUTED		M.	an individual who hates people
O	14. CYNICAL		N.	done beforehand or in preparation for
B	15. DIGNIFIED		O.	bitter and distrustful
I	16. DOTING		P.	sobriety; abstaining from drinking alcohol
A	17. ENGAGED		Q.	to cringe with fear
E	18. EXPURGATIONS		R.	loose or careless; not strict
C	19. GOVERNESS		S.	composed or constructed of
J	20. VACILLATING		T.	an expression of regret for doing something wrong

VOCABULARY JUGGLE LETTERS 1 - *The Importance of Being Earnest*

_____ = 1. LIINGVAATLC
indecisive or wavering

_____ = 2. TEYDERIARH
can be passed from an individual to his or her offspring

_____ = 3. ITNNADGIN
disgusted or annoyed

_____ = 4. LDINVIA
a person who is in frequently in poor health

_____ = 5. XAL
loose or careless; not strict

_____ = 6. RIEOCTMAADLM
overemotional and theatrical

_____ = 7. PIENHTAMROS
an individual who hates people

_____ = 8. OALUSTOENISTYT
in a showy manner; extravagantly

_____ = 9. PIENAYMRRIL
done beforehand or in preparation for

_____ = 10. AULIQ
to cringe with fear

_____ = 11. ERENAPENCT
an expression of regret for doing something wrong

_____ = 12. SNEIETMTN
an emotion or feeling

_____ = 13. EPCMEARETN
sobriety; abstaining from drinking alcohol

_____ = 14. TELAGTEU
protection or care by a guardian or tutor

_____ = 15. ESORSVENG
a female who lives with and teaches children in a private home

VOCABULARY JUGGLE LETTERS 1 ANSWER KEY - *The Importance of Being Earnest*

VACILLATING	= 1.	LIINGVAATLC
		indecisive or wavering
HEREDITARY	= 2.	TEYDERIARH
		can be passed from an individual to his or her offspring
INDIGNANT	= 3.	ITNNADGIN
		disgusted or annoyed
INVALID	= 4.	LDINVIA
		a person who is in frequently in poor health
LAX	= 5.	XAL
		loose or careless; not strict
MELODRAMATIC	= 6.	RIEOCTMAADLM
		overemotional and theatrical
MISANTHROPE	= 7.	PIENHTAMROS
		an individual who hates people
OSTENTATIOUSLY	= 8.	OALUSTOENISTYT
		in a showy manner; extravagantly
PRELIMINARY	= 9.	PIENAYMRRIL
		done beforehand or in preparation for
QUAIL	= 10.	AULIQ
		to cringe with fear
REPENTANCE	= 11.	ERENAPENCT
		an expression of regret for doing something wrong
SENTIMENT	= 12.	SNEIETMTN
		an emotion or feeling
TEMPERANCE	= 13.	EPCMEARETN
		sobriety; abstaining from drinking alcohol
TUTELAGE	= 14.	TELAGTEU
		protection or care by a guardian or tutor
GOVERNESS	= 15.	ESORSVENG
		a female who lives with and teaches children in a private home

VOCABULARY JUGGLE LETTERS 2 - *The Importance of Being Earnest*

_____	= 1.	ARUANTILIIT
		relating to usefulness instead of grace, beauty, or sophistication
_____	= 2.	AIPUCCSOA
		spacious or having the ability to hold a lot
_____	= 3.	CRMOEECM
		relating to trade or business
_____	= 4.	OTSMRIETNDAEV
		expressive or affectionate
_____	= 5.	LNPUERIASBE
		unable to be bypassed or overlooked
_____	= 6.	ALESIDVH
		given in abundance
_____	= 7.	ECHLNMLOYA
		depressing or spiritless
_____	= 8.	MLCPTYHAASEI
		abstract and philosophical
_____	= 9.	ORONUTIOS
		well-known for terrible reasons
_____	= 10.	RCTNHHPOLIAPI
		having to do with the giving of money or services to help others
_____	= 11.	ONPDGPNIOUR
		putting forth for others to consider
_____	= 12.	IYCALLRAD
		completely and thoroughly
_____	= 13.	LOSIYNTTNEESU
		self-righteously; expressing wise sayings and aphorisms
_____	= 14.	LIIYTTVRAI
		something unimportant and superficial
_____	= 15.	GMNEBICO
		attractive or flattering

VOCABULARY JUGGLE LETTERS 2 ANSWER KEY - *The Importance of Being Earnest*

UTILITARIAN	= 1.	ARUANTILIIT	
		relating to usefulness instead of grace, beauty, or sophistication	
CAPACIOUS	= 2.	AIPUCCSOA	
		spacious or having the ability to hold a lot	
COMMERCE	= 3.	CRMOEECM	
		relating to trade or business	
DEMONSTRATIVE	= 4.	OTSMRIETNDAEV	
		expressive or affectionate	
INSUPERABLE	= 5.	LNPUERIASBE	
		unable to be bypassed or overlooked	
LAVISHED	= 6.	ALESIDVH	
		given in abundance	
MELANCHOLY	= 7.	ECHLNMLOYA	
		depressing or spiritless	
METAPHYSICAL	= 8.	MLCPTYHAASEI	
		abstract and philosophical	
NOTORIOUS	= 9.	ORONUTIOS	
		well-known for terrible reasons	
PHILANTHROPIC	= 10.	RCTNHHPOLIAPI	
		having to do with the giving of money or services to help others	
PROPOUNDING	= 11.	ONPDGPNIOUR	
		putting forth for others to consider	
RADICALLY	= 12.	IYCALLRAD	
		completely and thoroughly	
SENTENTIOUSLY	= 13.	LOSIYNTTNEESU	
		self-righteously; expressing wise sayings and aphorisms	
TRIVIALITY	= 14.	LIIYTTVRAI	
		something unimportant and superficial	
BECOMING	= 15.	GMNEBICO	
		attractive or flattering	

www.ingramcontent.com/pod-product-compliance
Lightning Source LLC
Chambersburg PA
CBHW051406070526
44584CB00023B/3313